MBA Management Models

To Ann, Joanna and Jonathan.
TL

To Richard.
SH

MBA Management
Models

Sue Harding and Trevor Long

Gower

First published 1998 in hardback

Paperback edition published in 1998 by
Gower Publishing Limited
Gower House
Croft Road
Aldershot
Hampshire GU11 3HR
England

Gower Publishing Company
Suite 420, 101 Cherry Street
Burlington, VT 05401–4405
USA

Reprinted 2000, 2001, 2003

Sue Harding and Trevor Long have asserted their right under the Copyright, Designs and Patents Act 1988 to be identified as the authors of this work.

British Library Cataloguing in Publication Data
Harding, Sue
  Proven management models
  1. Industrial management – Mathematical models
  I.Title II. Long, Trevor
  658.4'033

  ISBN 0–566–07674–8

Library of Congress Cataloging-in-Publication Data
Harding, Sue
  Proven management models/Sue Harding and Trevor Long.
    p. cm
  Includes index.
  ISBN 0–566–07674–8
  1. Management. 2. Industrial management. I. Long, Trevor, 1956–
    II. Title
  HD31.H3195 1996   96–8726
  658—dc20   CIP

Typeset in 12 point Palatino by Bournemouth Colour Press
Printed and bound in Great Britain by
MPG Books Ltd, Bodmin, Cornwall

Contents

Human resources

Organizational strategy

Strategic marketing

Acknowledgements

The authors would like to thank Kim Anderson for her administrative assistance in the production of this book, and Colin Guest for his feedback on drafts.

SH
TL

Introduction

The aim of this book is to provide a summary of those models from management literature most often used in student assignments, management activities and business consultancy.

Selection of models

We have not sought to include every possible model. Our criteria for selection were:

- those models which most often help, and are expected to be used, in written student assignments, projects, case studies or dissertations
- those generic models which provide the most useful conceptual framework on which to build more specific and detailed understanding
- those models which are most useful in relation to the normal activities of today's organizations
- models which are included in most higher-level management courses.

Within this framework the selection is inevitably subjective. Readers may feel that a certain model which they consider crucial is missing whereas another which they consider as peripheral is included. Nevertheless we are confident that the broad scope of models is appropriate for the readers we have in mind.

Readership

This book will be useful to several types of reader:

1

- students on management education and training courses, including MBA and DMS programmes
- students on other courses which include business, organization or management units
- former students who wish to keep reference of main concepts they have studied and also wish to keep up-to-date with current ideas
- practising managers who wish to apply a more rigorous approach in their work
- consultants concerned with management or business.

Keeping the right focus

If you have not studied the principles behind different models, this book will help you identify the scope of problems that the application of models could tackle. However, we do not aim to give all the information needed by most readers to use a model effectively. The book is therefore not intended to provide a short-cut to study or problem solving. For students, it should not take the place of primary course texts, but complement and support them. Study of the primary literature, which gives the background, development and context within which a model may be applied, is still necessary.

We must be careful how we perceive models and their use. It is tempting to concentrate so heavily on a model's structure and workings that its real purpose, as an aid to answering broader questions, is forgotten. Rather than study a model and its uses in isolation we should always keep in mind the particular problem or assignment, and apply those models which help to answer questions that arise. Models should be used as tools to assist in specific research, analysis or development. They will not provide answers themselves, but will help to focus, direct and structure thinking and analysis.

Scope of models

The term 'model' is often used to describe a *pictorial* summary of principal issues within a particular domain. We feel that this description is too constraining and have chosen instead to include in this book models, frameworks, acronyms, listings and other summaries which we believe will meet the needs of the types of reader we have described. The basis for our selection has been not whether the summary can *strictly* be termed a 'model', but whether it satisfies our main selection criteria.

The main subject areas covered are:

- accounting/economics.
- business strategy
- human resources
- organizational strategy
- strategic marketing

The models are grouped under these main headings and are also listed alphabetically in the matrix index.

Some of the most important models in the area of finance, operations and other organizational functions are also included.

In most cases the models included are strategic in nature. Many models which deal with more specific operational or detailed issues are omitted.

Integration of models

You might wish to locate one model and apply it in isolation for a specific purpose. However, by their nature, many models focus on an organizational domain which, in reality, integrates and relates to other domains. And in a student assignment, analyses of different organizational issues should normally be integrated.

The models in this book are presented in a way which facilitates their use either individually or in a more integrated approach. For each model cross-references are given to related models. These could be used to extend a particular analysis or to develop it into other areas. We hope that this integrated approach will help students and managers to increase their creativity and the breadth of analysis in their work.

The nature of models

A model is a *representation* of reality. It seeks to encompass all the essential elements of a particular domain but, in so doing, it simplifies and generalizes. A model is a framework, identifying the broadest issues and considerations.

Models aim to clarify the *relationship* between different elements, indicating causal and effective interaction. They often try to show how a change in one part of a system or process may impact other parts. As such, a model is a *dynamic* representation of reality, demonstrating how different forces, from inside or outside the system, may change the whole.

Because models simplify reality they exclude specific consideration of particular issues. Whilst they aim to be all-encompassing, they cannot contain all the detailed elements required for a particular analysis. The most important issue might be a detail lying deep within the context of the framework offered by a model. Models should therefore be used not as a complete analysis in themselves but to help stimulate broader thinking about an area of interest in an analytical process.

The *general* nature of models can be problematic. In attempting to achieve a representation which is broadly applicable, models can sometimes appear to be simplistic, remote or theoretical. They may seek to describe the 'average' position – but what organization, problem or assignment is average? Models must not therefore be regarded as a complete and accurate *descriptive* tool. Because they cannot, in themselves, be relied on to capture all the crucial elements of a particualr situation, they should be used primarily to direct the main focus for analysis.

Models, once established in the literature and in management courses, can sometimes take on a timeless life of their own. Many models still being taught and appied today were introduced two, three or four decades ago. This is not to suggest they are no longer valid. But it *is* to suggest that their application should be critically assessed for a particular need in today's fast-changing organizational and business environment.

The representation of models

The models in this book are presented in a way that most effectively summarizes the interaction of main elements and usually follow the form produced by the original author. Each model is accompanied by explanatory text which is in seven sections:

- **Principle**: the basis or purpose of the model.
- **Assumptions**: underpinning ideas without which the model would not hold true.
- **Elements**: a descripton or definition of the identifiable parts of the model.
- **Issues**: a summary of significant topics or points intended to give further explanation and ideas concerning the context and analysis of the model.
- **Applications**: how the model may be used. For some models, applications which were not intended from the original development but which could produce a more creative analytical approach in a particular domain are included.
- **Related models**: other models included in the book which are in some way connected and which may facilitate a broader analytical approach.
- **Main references**: the original reference or one which most effectively summarizes greater detail and background to the model.

Application of models

The need to start from the problem area, relating to individuals, groups or whole organizations and their environments, rather than start from the model and finding applications, is emphasized throughout this book. It is more effective to use the models to assist in analyses and problem solving rather than start with the models and try to find relevant applications.

Nevertheless, the models may be used to enhance creative thinking about applications extending beyond their established use in the literature. To this end, the models themselves may form the focus of discussion in a search for novel analyses and solutions. The book may therefore be used by students, managers and consultants as an aid in tackling a wide range of problem areas.

In a practical, organization-based context the models may be used at different stages of a project. During diagnostics they will help to highlight the broad range of issues and prevent too great an emphasis on one area. At this stage they can also help to structure diagnostics and provide frameworks for summarizing information. During analysis, models can assist in the critical assessment of the impact and interaction of different elements within the problem area. In developing conclusions, they are a useful aid in the clear presentation of findings and in showing findings clearly and the interrelationship of main factors affecting the outcome of recommendations.

For students, this book can help with assignments, case studies or open-book examinations. Students should never simply describe models or concepts from the literature unless specifically asked to do so; they should use them to help with analysis and structure of written work. In particular, they should be used for a given problem area to help identify the main issues, assess their impact and importance, and format a response. Most student assignments are improved by moving from descriptive discussion, where facts are noted, through analysis of the facts to a more critical or creative treatment of the material. Models can assist most effectively in the analytical, and critical and creative approaches.

In any problem, the application of models, as summary representations of concepts and ideas from the literature, can help to clarify thinking, structure analysis and formulate responses. This book is organized to act as a reminder or summary of models, and to assist in their creative application.

A more in-depth discussion on the use of models is given in the Appendix.

Matrix index

Consult models related to your chosen model to enhance understanding and extend your options.

You may wish to add further cross-references yourself to the matrix shown opposite.

Below is the self-referencing matrix showing which techniques cross-reference one another. The diagonal (a technique against itself) is shown as ■; an X marks a cross-reference.

	ACTION-CENTRED LEADERSHIP	ANSOFF'S BOX	BARRIERS AND PROFITABILITY	BCG MATRIX	BELBIN'S TEAM ROLES	BREAK-EVEN ANALYSIS	COMPANY POSITION/INDUSTRY ...	CONTRASTING CHARACTERISTICS ...	CULTURAL WEB	DEMAND AND SUPPLY	DYNAMICS OF RECIPE CHANGE	ECONOMIES OF SCALE	ELASTICITY	FINANCIAL RATIOS	FIVE FORCES	5 Ps FOR STRATEGY	FOUR ORGANIZATIONAL CULTURES	FOUR ROUTES TO STRATEGIC ADVANTAGE	GENERIC STRATEGIES	GEOBUSINESS MODEL	GROUP DEVELOPMENT	HERZBERG'S MOTIVATOR–HYGIENE THEORY	INTEGRATED MODEL OF STRATEGIC ...	INTERNAL RATE OF RETURN (IRR)	JOB CHARACTERISTICS	MANAGERIAL GRID	MASLOW'S HIERARCHY OF NEEDS	M-O-S-T	NET PRESENT VALUE (NPV)	NETWORK ANALYSIS, PERT, CPA	NINE SPECIMEN STANDARDIZED ...	ORGANIC VERSUS MECHANISTIC ...	PATTERNS OF STRATEGIC CHANGE	PESTLIED	PIMS COMPETITIVE STRATEGY PARADIGM	PORTER'S DIAMOND	PRODUCT LIFE CYCLE	RELATED DIVERSIFICATION GRID	RESOURCE ALLOCATION AT CORPORATE ...	THE SEVEN Ss FRAMEWORK	SITUATIONAL LEADERSHIP	STRATEGIC TRIANGLE	SWOT ANALYSIS	VALUE CHAIN	VARIANCE ANALYSIS
ACTION-CENTRED LEADERSHIP	■																																												
ANSOFF'S BOX		■																																											
BARRIERS AND PROFITABILITY			■																																										
BCG MATRIX		X		■																																									
BELBIN'S TEAM ROLES	X				■																																								
BREAK-EVEN ANALYSIS						■																																							
COMPANY POSITION/INDUSTRY ...		X	X		X		■																																						
CONTRASTING CHARACTERISTICS ...							X	■																																					
CULTURAL WEB	X				X				■																																				
DEMAND AND SUPPLY			X		X					■																																			
DYNAMICS OF RECIPE CHANGE									X		■																																		
ECONOMIES OF SCALE				X		X				X		■																																	
ELASTICITY				X		X				X			■																																
FINANCIAL RATIOS														■																															
FIVE FORCES		X	X				X						X		■																														
5 Ps FOR STRATEGY							X	X			X				X	■																													
FOUR ORGANIZATIONAL CULTURES					X				X	X							■																												
FOUR ROUTES TO STRATEGIC ADVANTAGE																X	X	■																											
GENERIC STRATEGIES								X								X		X	■																										
GEOBUSINESS MODEL											X					X				■																									
GROUP DEVELOPMENT					X				X									X			■																								
HERZBERG'S MOTIVATOR–HYGIENE THEORY	X				X				X													■																							
INTEGRATED MODEL OF STRATEGIC ...																X		X	X				■																						
INTERNAL RATE OF RETURN (IRR)						X					X													■																					
JOB CHARACTERISTICS	X																					X	X		■																				
MANAGERIAL GRID	X								X																	■																			
MASLOW'S HIERARCHY OF NEEDS					X																	X	X		X	X	■																		
M-O-S-T											X																X	■																	
NET PRESENT VALUE (NPV)						X					X													X					■																
NETWORK ANALYSIS, PERT, CPA			X																					X						■															
NINE SPECIMEN STANDARDIZED ...			X				X	X			X				X		X	X	X			X			X			X			■														
ORGANIC VERSUS MECHANISTIC ...								X		X					X		X	X	X				X			X		X	X			■													
PATTERNS OF STRATEGIC CHANGE																	X	X					X			X					X		■												
PESTLIED								X								X				X			X								X			■											
PIMS COMPETITIVE STRATEGY PARADIGM								X						X					X															X	■										
PORTER'S DIAMOND								X							X	X		X	X											X			X			■									
PRODUCT LIFE CYCLE	X	X	X						X						X												X	X				X		X	X		■								
RELATED DIVERSIFICATION GRID							X	X																											X	X		■							
RESOURCE ALLOCATION AT CORPORATE ...																																			X	X			■						
THE SEVEN Ss FRAMEWORK				X				X	X	X							X	X					X					X	X							X				■				X	
SITUATIONAL LEADERSHIP	X			X				X								X					X	X			X	X	X				X										■			X	
STRATEGIC TRIANGLE								X							X		X	X	X						X				X			X			X	X						■		X	
SWOT ANALYSIS				X		X		X							X		X	X	X			X						X			X											X	■	X	
VALUE CHAIN			X		X	X							X									X					X										X						X	■	
VARIANCE ANALYSIS										X		X																																	■

9

Accounting/economics

1 Break-even analysis

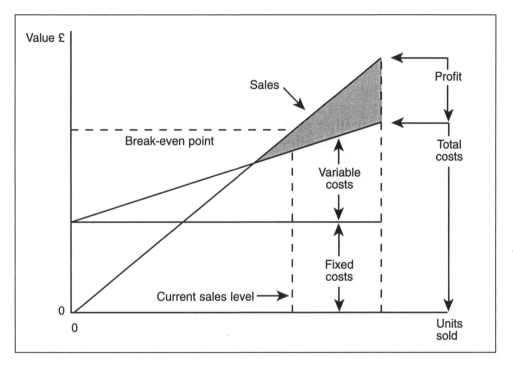

Source: *Finance for the Non-Financial Manager*, J. Harrison/Lucas Productions, HarperCollins, London, 1989.

Principle

Break-even analysis is a marginal costing technique which is used to identify how total costs, revenues and profits are related to sales volume.

Assumptions

Because unit variable costs and total fixed costs are constant, for one additional unit of production, costs will rise only by the marginal (variable) cost of production and sales for that unit.

Additional profit earned by that extra unit is equal to unit contribution (revenue less marginal cost for that unit).

Elements

Break-even point
The break-even point occurs where revenues and total costs are equal so there is neither profit nor loss. It is expressed as number of units sold or amount of sales revenue.

Revenues, sales revenue
Revenues are the financial income from the sale of the units.

Total costs
These comprise the total of variable (marginal) costs plus fixed costs.

Issues

CPV
Break-even analysis is also known as cost-volume-profit analysis (CPV),

Conditions
Conditions under which the model is reliable are as follows:

- the sales price per unit should be constant
- stock levels should not vary significantly, so production sales volumes should be equal
- the sales mix should be constant at all levels of activity

- the model is applied within the organization's normal range of output levels.

Fixed costs
Fixed costs may actually be step costs over a wide range of activity.

Applications

Forecasting
The model may be used to identify how total costs, revenues and profits are related to sales volume. Break-even analysis may then be used to forecast the effects on profit of changes in costs and sales volume.

Budget planning
Break-even analysis may be applied within budget planning by calculating the volume of sales required to break even and the safety margin for profits in the budget.

Decision-making
The model aids decision-making relating to sales mix, cost structure and production capacity.

Related models

- **Company position/industry attractiveness screen** (see pp. 137–140)
- **Demand and supply** (see pp. 17–20)
- **Economies of scale** (see pp. 21–4)
- **Elasticity** (see pp. 25–8)
- **Internal rate of return** (IRR) (see pp. 33–6)
- **M-O-S-T** (see pp. 161–3)

Main reference

J. Harrison/Lucas Productions (1989), *Finance for the Non-Financial Manager*, London: HarperCollins.

2 Demand and supply

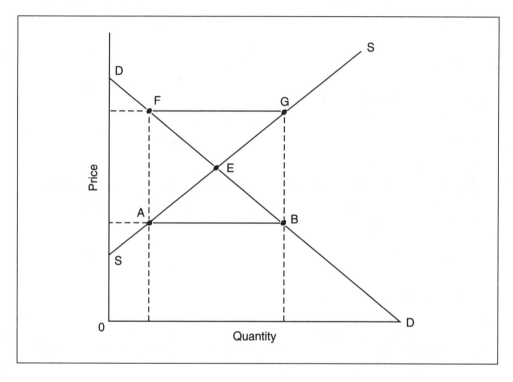

Source: *Economics, Third Edition*, D. Begg, S. Fischer and R. Dornbusch, McGraw-Hill, Maidenhead, 1991. Copyright © David Begg, 1991.

Principle

Demand is the quantity of goods that buyers wish to purchase at a stated price.

Supply is the quantity of goods that sellers wish to sell at a stated price.

Assumption

Other things being equal, the lower the price the higher the quantity of goods demanded and the lower the quantity supplied.

Elements

Demand and supply curves
Demand curves (D–D) slope downwards; supply curves (S–S) slope upwards.

Equilibrium
The market is in equilibrium when the price equates quantity demanded with quantity supplied – that is, where demand and supply curves intersect at E.

Issues

Constraints on the model
The demand curve assumes that prices of other goods, incomes and fashions or tastes remain constant. The supply curve assumes that technology, price of inputs and degree of government regulation remain constant.

Equilibrium
At prices below equilibrium price E there is excess demand AB (shortage) which tends to raise price. At prices above equilibrium price there is excess supply FG (surplus) which tends to reduce price.

Substitutes and complements
An increase in the price of a substitute or a decrease in the price of a complement raises quantity demanded.

Increased demand and supply
A factor that increases demand shifts the demand curve to the right, increasing price and quantity demanded. A factor that increases supply shifts the supply curve to the right, reducing price but increasing quantity supplied.

Price ceiling
An effective price ceiling may be set below the market equilibrium price to reduce quantity supplied and create excess demand until, or unless, the government contributes to supply.

Price floor
An effective price floor may be set above market equilibrium price to increase quantity supplied and so depress demand until, or unless, the government makes up the demand shortfall itself through orders.

Applications

Price setting
The model can assist in price setting (supply price or purchase price) and, hence, costing.

Predicting responses to price changes
The model may be used to predict the likely response of suppliers or customers to changes in price that the organization is willing to pay or intends to charge customers.

Optimal levels of supply
A supplier may calculate optimal levels of goods to supply to customers to give the best return.

Avoiding surplus
Supplier organizations may predict market equilibrium prices and so set a price which avoids being left with a surplus but, instead, stimulates demand.

Dictating supplier prices
With a knowledge of market equilibrium price, purchasing organizations with large spending power may dictate supplier price – for example, by purchasing from another source until the original supplier's prices fall.

Related models

- **Barriers and profitability** (see pp. 47–50)
- **Break-even analysis** (see pp. 13–16)
- **Economies of scale** (see pp. 21–4)
- **Elasticity** (see pp. 25–8)
- **Internal rate of return** (IRR) (see pp. 33–6)
- **Net present value** (NPV) (see pp. 37–40)
- **SWOT analysis** (see pp. 187–90)

Main reference

D. Begg, S. Fischer and R. Dornbusch (1991), *Economics*, (3rd edn), Maidenhead: McGraw-Hill Book Company Europe.

3 Economies of scale

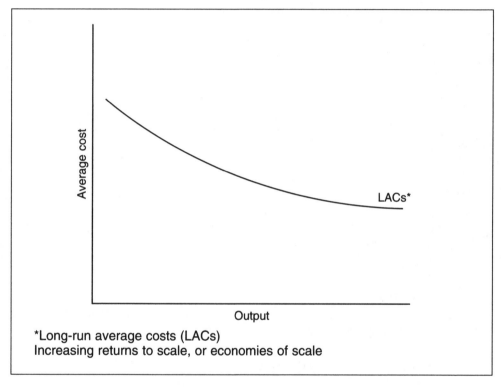

*Long-run average costs (LACs)
Increasing returns to scale, or economies of scale

Principle

Economies of scale are increasing returns which are achieved when average costs (cost divided by output) decrease as output (the volume of production) rises.

Assumption

Economies of scale result when factors of production are used effectively as output rises.

Elements

LACs
When LACs (long-run average costs) are declining, average costs of production fall as output increases and economies of scale are achieved.

Issues

Constant returns to scale
Constant returns to scale occur when long-run average costs remain unchanged as output rises.

Diseconomies of scale
Diseconomies of scale, or decreasing returns, are achieved when long-run average costs increase as output rises.

Reasons for economies of scale
These include:

- indivisibilities in the production process, such as fixed costs
- specialization, where outputs increase through expertise and efficiency
- better plant and equipment within larger organizations.

Diseconomies of scale
These are usually:

- managerial, when large organizations become bureaucratic
- location-based, if no readily available workforce/market exists
- due to diminishing returns when, beyond some level of variable input such as labour or equipment, further increases in input lead to diminishing marginal returns through overstaffing or underutilization, respectively.

Organizational staffing
Flatter organizational staff structures mean lower management staffing levels. This reduces costs and bureaucracy, but can only result in economies of scale if the remaining managers control their increased responsibilities effectively. Further, the decision whether to encourage staff to specialize or to multitask should depend upon the requirements of the particular business unit.

Applications

Targeting economies
Potential economies of scale within an organization may be identified and targeted to increase profitability.

Calculation of optimum output levels
Output levels may be calculated to optimise economies of scale.

Other uses
Appreciation of economies of scale stimulates:

- fixed cost control
- job design, promoting specialization where appropriate
- more efficient utilization of plant and labour
- careful appraisal of managerial effectiveness.

Related models

- **BCG matrix** (see pp. 51–4)
- **Break-even analysis** (see pp. 13–16)
- **Demand and supply** (see pp. 17–20)
- **Geobusiness model** (see pp. 77–81)
- **Nine specimen standardized strategies** (see pp. 201–5)
- **Product life cycle** (see pp. 211–14)
- **Strategic triangle** (see pp. 95–8)
- **Variance analysis** (see pp. 41–4)

Main reference

D. Begg, S. Fischer and R. Dornbusch (1991), *Economics*, (3rd edn), Maidenhead: McGraw-Hill Book Company Europe.

4 Elasticity

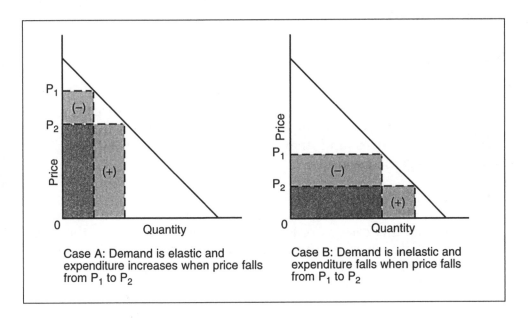

Case A: Demand is elastic and expenditure increases when price falls from P_1 to P_2

Case B: Demand is inelastic and expenditure falls when price falls from P_1 to P_2

Source: *Economics, Third Edition*, D. Begg, S. Fischer and R. Dornbusch, McGraw-Hill, Maidenhead, 1991. Copyright © David Begg, 1991.

Principle

Elasticity measures the sensitivity of demand or supply of goods to percentage changes in the price of those goods (price elasticity) or to changes in the income available to purchase those goods (income elasticity).

Assumptions

Quantities of goods demanded and supplied vary with changes in prices of those goods, changes in prices of other related goods and changes in available income. When price falls from P_1 to P_2 (see diagram), income is lost through fall in price [(−)] and gained through increase in quantity [(+)].

Elements

Elasticity
Price elasticity of demand (sensitivity of demand to price) is elastic if price elasticity is more negative than −1. This means that demand falls as price rises and that price cuts increase total spending (demand) on the goods.

Inelasticity
Price elasticity of demand is inelastic if demand elasticity is between −1 and 0. In this case, people buy fewer of the goods as the price falls, as if price were an indicator of quality or desirability, so that price cuts reduce total spending (demand) on the goods.

Issues

Demand elasticities
Demand elasticities are zero or negative.

Supply elasticities
Supply elasticities are zero or positive.

Inferior goods
Inferior goods have negative income elasticities of demand because high incomes reduce quantity demanded and budget share of such goods.

Luxury goods
Luxury goods normally have income elasticities larger than 1.

Necessities
Necessities have positive income elasticities of demand (more than 0 but less than 1).

Cross-price elasticities
Cross-price elasticities of demand or supply measure sensitivity of quantity of goods demanded or supplied to changes in the price of related goods. For example, substitutes (such as sugar and artificial sweeteners) have positive cross-price elasticities of demand, while complementary goods (such as computers and floppy disks) have negative cross-price elasticities of demand.

Applications

Price setting
The model may serve as an aid in price setting (supply price or purchase price) and, hence, costing.

Predicting responses to price changes
The model may be used to predict likely response of suppliers or customers to changes in price that the organization is willing to pay, or intends to charge, customers.

Optimal levels of supply
A supplier may use the model to calculate optimal levels of goods to supply to customers to yield the best return.

New markets or products
An appreciation of elasticity assists in making decisions regarding entry into new markets or launching new products.

Related models

- **BCG matrix** (see pp. 51–4)
- **Break-even analysis** (see pp. 13–16)
- **Demand and supply** (see pp. 17–20)
- **Five forces** (see pp. 59–63)
- **PIMS competitive strategy paradigm** (see pp. 207–10)
- **Porter's Diamond** (see pp. 87–90)

Main reference

D. Begg, S. Fischer and R. Dornbusch (1991), *Economics*, (3rd edn), Maidenhead: McGraw-Hill Book Company Europe.

5 Financial ratios

Liquidity ratios:

Current Ratio $= \dfrac{\text{Current Assets}}{\text{Current Liabilities}}$

Acid Test Ratio $= \dfrac{\text{Current Assets less Stock}}{\text{Current Liabilities}}$

Profitability ratios:

Gross Profit to Sales $= \dfrac{\text{Gross Profit x 100}}{\text{Sales}}$

Net Profit to Sales $= \dfrac{\text{Net Profit x 100}}{\text{Sales}}$

Use of assets ratios:

Debtors' Collection Period $= \dfrac{\text{Debtors x 365}}{\text{Sales}}$

Sales to Fixed Assets $= \dfrac{\text{Sales}}{\text{Fixed assets}}$

Capital structure ratios:

Gearing Ratio $= \dfrac{\text{Debt}}{\text{Share Capital}}$

Interest Cover $= \dfrac{\text{Profit before Interest and Tax}}{\text{Interest Paid}}$

Investors' returns ratios:

Earnings per share $= \dfrac{\text{Profit after Tax and Preference Share Dividend}}{\text{Number of Issued Ordinary Shares}}$

Dividend Cover $= \dfrac{\text{Profit after Tax less Preference Dividend}}{\text{Gross Dividend on Ordinary Shares}}$

Principle

The model describes several key financial and accounting ratios.

Assumption

Ratios are useful assessment and comparative tools when appraising and comparing results of different organizations or business units.

Elements and issues

Current ratio
This should be in the region of 2:1 or 1:1 to reflect a healthy proportion of current assets (cash, stock, debtors) to current liabilities (overdraft, creditors).

Acid test ratio
This is a stricter test of liquidity than the current ratio because it compares money and potential money assets (cash and debtors) to current liabilities.

Gross profit and net profit to sales
Both these profitability percentage ratios should show an increase over time as the organization becomes established. There tend to be industry 'norm' ranges – for example, profit percentage might be expected to be lower in a given manufacturing industry than in a stated service industry.

Debtor's collection period
This ratio shows how long debtors take to pay. There tend to be industry 'norms'. For example, in some industries the custom is to permit three months' credit but in others, payment within 30 days is expected. Every organization is at liberty to try to improve its debtors' collection period whatever the industry 'norm'.

Sales to fixed assets
Sales should be greater than fixed assets. The larger the differential, the better is the organization using its assets.

Gearing ratio
The more long-term debt funding, the higher is the gearing and the greater is the risk incurred. Gearing is said to be high at figures above 1:1.

Interest cover
The higher the ratio, the less risk is involved as interest paid becomes a small proportion of profit.

Earnings per share
High earnings per share encourage new investors and promote existing investor loyalty.

Dividend cover
High dividend cover is healthy provided that the investor judges the gross dividend on ordinary shares to be adequate. A high dividend cover may indicate that the Board of Directors is being ungenerous to investors. Low dividend cover may indicate that gross dividends on ordinary shares have been set too high.

Comparisons should be of like with like. For example, comparing the results of organizations in different industries would probably be of little value.

Applications

Interfirm or inter-unit comparisons
The ratios facilitate comparisons between the results of different organizations or business units.

Targeting
With knowledge of what the ideal range of ratio results should be

for a given industry organizations and business units can target improvements. For example, if net profit to sales is too low, the organization can assess whether sales can realistically be increased and/or whether expenses need tighter control (to increase net profit).

Audit
The ratios are a valuable tool for auditors who can use them to compare expected results with actual results and investigate differences.

Related models

- **Organic versus mechanistic management styles** (see pp. 169–72)
- **SWOT analysis** (see pp. 187–90)
- **Value chain** (see pp. 191–4)
- **Variance analysis** (see pp. 41–4)

Main reference

Financial accounting textbooks in general.

6 Internal rate of return (IRR)

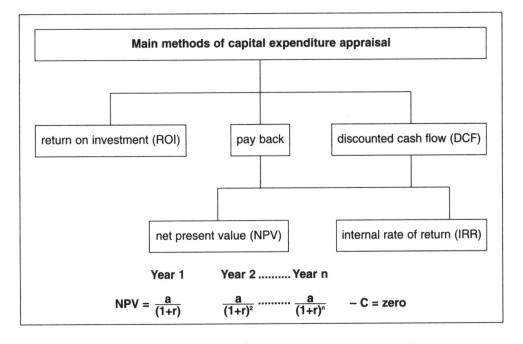

Source: *Finance for the Non-Financial Manager*, J. Harrison/Lucas Productions, HarperCollins, London, 1989.

Principle

There is a yardstick for the appraisal of capital expenditure based on discounted cash flow methods.

IRR is the earning rate of the capital sum to be expended at which the net present value (NPV) is zero.

Assumptions

Capital expenditure projects calculated to give an IRR in excess of current or target interest rates are attractive.

Money has a time value because of investment opportunities, consumers' eagerness to spend and anticipated inflation. Thus, money held in the present is of greater value than cash due to be received in the future.

Elements

IRR
IRR is the earning rate of the capital sum to be expended at which the net present value is zero.

NPV
NPV is equal to the estimated increase in the value of the firm's future cash flows stated at present cash values.

- **a:** estimated cash flows at the end of each year, reduced to current values
- **r:** IRR expressed as a decimal
- **C:** the project or investment cost payable immediately

Issues

Discount rate
IRR equals the discount rate at which the present value of all future cash flows, positive and negative, is equal to the cost of the capital expenditure or project.

Viability of project
IRR determines whether the return on capital expenditure is more or less than that achieved by investing that sum at current or target investment interest rates and so assists, for example, in making a

decision whether to purchase premises as opposed to investing those same funds at current forecast interest rates.

Other considerations
An attractive internal rate of return alone may be insufficient justification for the capital project to proceed. Other, non-financial factors may warrant consideration, such as location, and availability of a workforce in relation to premises to be purchased.

Use of tables
The IRR is usually found by trial and error using different percentage return/NPV tables until a near zero percentage is reached.

Applications

Appraisal
The model helps with capital expenditure appraisal (projects, investments) and aids considerations of risk and return.

Management
Consideration of IRR facilitates management of fixed assets.

Decision making
IRR assists informed lease/buy decisions and decision-making concerning additional capacity

Related models

- **Break-even analysis** (see pp. 13–16)
- **Demand and supply** (see pp. 17–20)
- **Net present value (NPV)** (see pp. 37–40)

Main references

J. Harrison (1989), *Finance for the Non-Financial Manager*, London: HarperCollins.

J. Arnold and T. Hope (1990), *Accounting for Management Decisions*, London: Prentice Hall International (UK) Ltd.

7   Net present value (NPV)

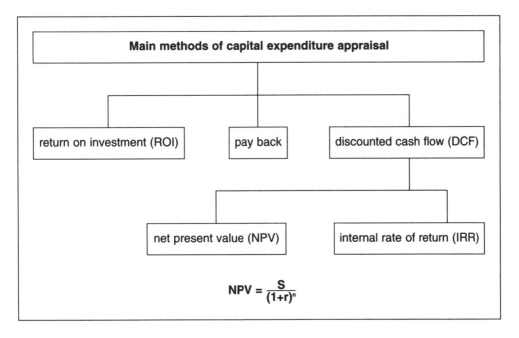

Main methods of capital expenditure appraisal

return on investment (ROI)   pay back   discounted cash flow (DCF)

net present value (NPV)   internal rate of return (IRR)

$$NPV = \frac{S}{(1+r)^n}$$

Source: Finance for the Non-Financial Manager, J. Harrison/Lucas Productions, HarperCollins, London, 1989.

Principle

NPV is a yardstick for appraising capital expenditure projects based on discounted cash flow methods.

It is equal to the estimated increase in the value of the firm's future cash flows stated at present cash values.

Assumptions

A capital expenditure project that is calculated to give a positive NPV return is an attractive project.

Money has a time value because of investment opportunities, consumers' eagerness to spend and anticipated inflation. Thus, money held in the present is of greater value than cash due to be received in the future.

Elements

NPV
NPV is equal to the estimated increase in the value of the firm's future cash flows stated at present cash values.

- **S**: the estimated future sum to be received
- **r**: the rate of interest, expressed as a decimal, that could be received if the capital expenditure funds were invested instead
- **n**: the number of years in the future at which S, the future sum, is expected to be received.

Issues

Decision-making
NPV determines whether the return on capital expenditure is more or less than that achieved by investing that sum at current investment interest rates. For example, NPV will assist in deciding whether to purchase equipment or invest those same funds at current forecast interest rates.

Positive and negative NPV
A positive NPV indicates that the capital expenditure will increase the firm's value. A negative NPV indicates the reverse.

Other factors
Positive financial returns alone may be insufficient justification for the capital project to proceed. Other, non-financial factors, such as performance and reliability of plant to be purchased, may also warrant consideration.

Timing and estimating
Accurate timing and estimating of future cash flows is difficult because of tax payments.

Current values
When calculating NPV, all estimated future cash flows must first be reduced to current values.

Year zero
Initial capital expenditure is assumed to occur at year zero.

Use of tables
Tables which give the standard discount factors for NPV by discount rate percentage may be used.

Applications

Appraisal
The model assists with capital expenditure appraisal (projects, investments) and aids in the consideration of risk and return.

Management
Consideration of NPV facilitates management of fixed assets.

Decision-making
NPV assists informed lease/buy decision-making and decision-making with regard to additional capacity.

Related models

- **Break-even analysis** (see pp. 13–16)
- **Demand and supply** (see pp. 17–20)
- **Internal rate of return** (IRR) (see pp. 33–6)
- **Network analysis, PERT, CPA** (see pp. 165–8)

Main references

J. Harrison (1989), *Finance for the Non-Financial Manager*, London: HarperCollins.

J. Arnold and T. Hope (1990), *Accounting for Management Decisions*, London: Prentice Hall International (UK) Ltd.

8 Variance analysis

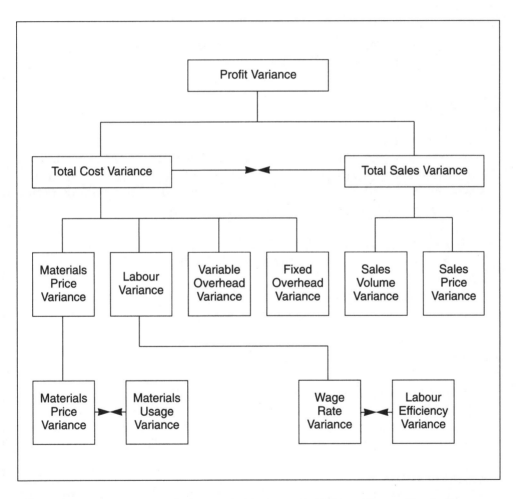

Source: *Finance for the Non-Financial Manager*, J. Harrison/Lucas Productions, HarperCollins, London, 1989.

Principle

Variance analysis is the analysis of differences between actual and planned performance (variances).

Assumption

The differences between actual and planned performance can be explained by analysing variances.

Elements

Variance analysis
Variance analysis commences with the splitting of main variances into their component parts to locate precisely where and why the variance has actually occurred. For example, a sales variance (sales results better or worse than planned) comprises:

Sales price variance = (actual price – planned price) x actual volume of sales achieved

and

Sales volume variance = (actual volume – planned volume) x planned sales price

Issues

Positive and negative variances
Variances are unfavourable, adverse or negative if they lead to worse performance results than planned. Variances are favourable or positive if they lead to better performance results than planned.

Order of response
Managers tend to locate the cause of the largest or most significant variance first and to analyse only the most costly variances.

Small variances
Small variances in unit costs or unit prices can have significant effects when accompanied by large volumes.

Causes of variances
Causes of variances include inefficiency, poor communication and/or setting of plans and standards, random fluctuations and interdependence of departments.

Appraisal
By identifying volume variances and revising budget volumes accordingly (budget revision variances), managers' forecasting and planning skills may be evaluated. Variances between the revised budget and actual results then become control variances which show whether managers have achieved optimum results following budget revision.

Standard costing system
If an effective standard costing system is in place, variances will be minimized, more easily investigated and correctly attributed to responsibility centres.

Costs versus benefits of investigation
Before investigating variances it is advisable to ensure that the cost of so doing is justified by the likely benefits/savings.

Applications

Performance evaluation
The model helps in the evaluation of manager, business unit and company performance.

Improving performance
Understanding the causes of variances enables the manager to recreate or avoid such variances in future and so improve performance.

Control and quality
Variance analysis can reduce inefficiency and improve planning and standards setting.

Reporting
Variance analysis permits identification and reporting of organizational activities which are not proceeding to plan or are performing above standard.

Related models

- **Economies of scale** (see pp. 21–4)
- **Financial ratios** (see pp. 29–32)

Main references

J. Harrison (1989), *Finance for the Non-Financial Manager*, London: Guild Publishing.

J. Arnold and T. Hope (1990), *Accounting for Management Decisions*, London: Prentice Hall Int. (UK) Ltd.

M. Bromwich (1980), *Standard Costing for Planning and Control*, Hemel Hempstead: Philip Allan.

Business strategy

9 Barriers and profitability

	EXIT BARRIERS	
	LOW	**HIGH**
ENTRY BARRIERS **LOW**	PROFITS=LOW RETURNS=STABLE	PROFITS=LOW RETURNS=RISKY
HIGH	PROFITS=HIGH RETURNS=STABLE	PROFITS=HIGH RETURNS=RISKY

Adapted with the permission of The Free Press, a division of Simon & Schuster from *COMPETITIVE STRATEGY: Techniques for Analyzing Industries and Competitors*, by Michael E. Porter. Copyright © 1980 by The Free Press.

Principle

The model shows how organizations' returns vary with the strength of market exit and entry barriers.

Assumption

The magnitude of organizations' returns depends significantly upon the strength of market exit and entry barriers.

Elements

Exit barriers

- specialized assets such as low liquidation values
- fixed costs of exit – for example, redundancy payments
- strategic interrelationships and alliances
- emotional barriers – for example, fear of unemployment
- government and social restrictions

Entry barriers

- economies of scale, such as bulk purchasing
- product differentiation, such as branding
- capital requirement – for example, research and development
- supplier switching costs
- access to distribution channels
- cost disadvantages independent of scale, such as technology and good location
- government policy – for example, industry regulation

Issues

Best position
High entry barriers with low exit barriers can be the best position for the established organization. In this way, high, stable returns can be achieved, and unsuccessful firms may readily exit the market.

Worst position
The worst position for organizations can be in a market exhibiting

low entry barriers and high exit barriers. New entrants are attracted into the market by upturns in the economy but cannot leave when conditions deteriorate. This leads to poor profits caused by surplus capacity.

Changes to barriers
Entry barriers, in particular, can change over time due to, for example, expiry of patents and licensing agreements, the formation of strategic alliances and the organization's developing skill.

Applications

Lateral thinking
Understanding of the model promotes outward thinking and an understanding of the environment in which the organization operates and competes.

Predicting behaviour
The model may be used to predict competitor behaviour with regard to a new or existing market, given existing entry and exit barriers.

Selecting markets
The model may be used to help the organization select markets that will give better returns with the desired order of risk.

Choice of markets
The audit and improved control of entry and exit barrier features impinging upon the organization (such as fixed costs of exit, access to distribution channels or economies of scale) gives it a wider choice of markets.

Related models

- **Company position/industry attractiveness screen** (see pp. 137–40)
- **Demand and supply** (see pp. 17–20)
- **Five forces** (see pp. 59–63)
- **Nine specimen standardized strategies** (see pp. 201–5)

Main reference

Michael E. Porter (1980), *Competitive Strategy – Techniques for Analyzing Industries and Competitors*, New York: The Free Press.

10 BCG Matrix

Market Share

		High	Low
Market Growth Rate	High	Star	Question mark (or problem child)
	Low	Cash cow	Dog

Source: *The Logic of Business Strategy*, Ballinger Publishing, New York, 1984.

Principle

This model defines particular product types within an organization's product portfolio.

Assumption

Market growth rate and market share affect the profitability and cash generation potential of products.

Elements

Stars
These are self-financing, cash-generating products, enjoying economies of scale and falling unit costs.

Question marks
Such products require more cash input to sustain them in a growing market than they can generate.

Cash cows
These products generate more cash than can be profitably reinvested in them. Unit costs are falling.

Dogs
Dogs are a drain on cash flow and may monopolize resources.

Issues

Product position
A company can increase market share and exploit market growth rate in order to move into a more attractive product position – for example, from dog position to star.

Investment
Higher marketing investment would normally be required for question marks (low market share) than for cash cows or stars.

Experience
The model relates to the 'experience curve'. As experience increases, the required amount of investment for product development decreases.

Competition
The importance of competitive forces must be assessed when

seeking to reposition products using this model.

Applications

Strategy evaluation
Managers may analyse the product portfolio to enhance strategy evaluation.

Resource allocation
Resources should be allocated appropriately to the type of product – for example, increase investment in question marks should be increased, investment in dogs should be decreased or stopped.

Encouraging growth
Market share and growth rate opportunities may be exploited through product portfolio planning to aim for stars (high profit), cash cows (cash generation) and question marks (future cash cows/stars).

As an analysis tool
The model may be used to analyse resources and other organizational factors in addition to products. For example, it is possible to classify staff, such as super salespersons, as stars or to evaluate equipment such as old, obsolete plant, as dogs.

Related models

- **Ansoff's Box** (see pp. 197–9)
- **Economies of scale** (see pp. 21–4)
- **Elasticity** (see pp. 25–8)
- **Network analysis, PERT, CPA** (see pp. 165–8)
- **Product life cycle** (see pp. 211–14)
- **Value chain** (see pp. 191–4)

Main reference

B. D. Henderson (1984), *The Logic of Business Strategy*, New York: Ballinger Publishing Co.

11 Contrasting characteristics of upstream and downstream companies

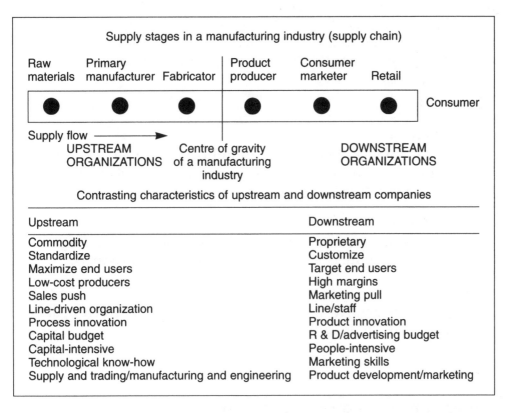

Supply stages in a manufacturing industry (supply chain)

Raw materials	Primary manufacturer	Fabricator	Product producer	Consumer marketer	Retail	
●	●	●	●	●	●	Consumer

Supply flow ———→

UPSTREAM ORGANIZATIONS

Centre of gravity of a manufacturing industry

DOWNSTREAM ORGANIZATIONS

Contrasting characteristics of upstream and downstream companies

Upstream	Downstream
Commodity	Proprietary
Standardize	Customize
Maximize end users	Target end users
Low-cost producers	High margins
Sales push	Marketing pull
Line-driven organization	Line/staff
Process innovation	Product innovation
Capital budget	R & D/advertising budget
Capital-intensive	People-intensive
Technological know-how	Marketing skills
Supply and trading/manufacturing and engineering	Product development/marketing

Reprinted by permission from page 51 of *Strategy Implementation – Structure, Systems and Process* by J.R. Galbraith and R.K. Kazanjian; Copyright © 1987 by West Publishing Company.

Principle

An organization's position in the supply flow of a manufacturing industry should determine its strategy and structure.

Assumptions

Performance is the product of many factors but mainly of matching strategy to industry structure and core skills and matching organizational structure to strategy.

The key to successful vertical integration is to support or maintain the firm's existing centre of gravity. Thus, any move upstream or downstream must be subordinate to its principal stage activities.

Elements

Upstream
Upstream organizations within an industry add value by reducing the variety of raw materials to a small number of materials and intermediate products.

Downstream
Downstream organizations convert these materials and intermediate products into a variety of consumer products.

Centre of gravity
The centre of gravity is defined as the position between upstream and downstream organizations within an industry.

Issues

Alignment of structure with strategy
To be successful, and to optimize competitive advantage, an organization should align structure with strategy. For example:

- Single business and dominant business firms should be organized in a functional structure.
- Related diversified firms should be organized into a multidivisional form.
- Unrelated diversified firms should be organised into a holding company structure.

Upstream versus downstream

Upstream and downstream organizations have contrasting characteristics. Upstream organizations normally have a divergent view of their environment; downstream organizations have a convergent view.

Centre of gravity

An organization may develop and move up or down the supply chain, but moving across the industry's centre of gravity is the most difficult strategy.

Added value

For downstream organizations value is added by advertising, product positioning, distribution and research and development.

Applications

Audit of the organization

The model may be used to audit the characteristics of an organization against stated upstream and downstream criteria.

Audit of the business unit

The model may be applied to assess upstream and downstream business units within a diversified organization.

Assessment and supply chain positioning

The model may be used to assess the organization's position within its industry's supply chain and to develop a strategy for moving along the supply chain (forward/backward integration).

Related models

- **Company position/industry attractiveness screen** (see pp. 137–40)
- **Five Ps for strategy** (see pp. 65–8)
- **Generic strategies** (see pp. 73–6)
- **Nine specimen standardized strategies** (see pp. 201–5)
- **The seven 'S's framework** (see pp. 181–5)
- **SWOT analysis** (see pp. 187–90)
- **Value chain** (see pp. 191–4)

Main reference

J.R. Galbraith and R.K. Kazanjian (1987), *Strategy Implementation – Structure, Systems and Process*, Minneapolis MN: West Publishing Co.

12 Five forces

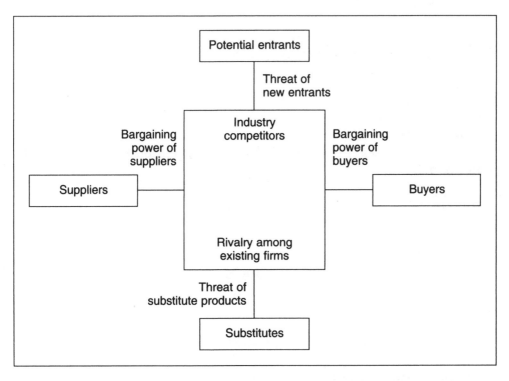

Principle

It is possible to classify forces acting against a firm into five main categories.

Assumption

The five forces can act continuously and adversely against the firm unless it defends itself or influences them in its favour.

Elements

Potential entrants
These are new players which threaten the livelihood of firms already in the market.

Buyers
Buyers are the customers of a firms products.

Substitutes
These are competitors' products (services) which may be alternatives to those supplied by the firm.

Suppliers
Suppliers provide raw materials and other resources.

Industry competitors
These are firms which compete in the same market and act as rivals to the organization.

Issues

Effect of the forces
The effect of the five forces upon organizations may vary depending

on the strength of the firm, the nature of the sector and the product.

Potential entrants
Potential entrants may be deterred by:

- economies of scale achieved by existing firms
- entrenched customer loyalty
- capital costs of entry (for example, plant and equipment)
- poor access to distribution channels
- cost disadvantages such as licences and adverse government policy.

Buyers
Buyers may try to force down prices whilst requiring better quality or service and may play off competitors against one another. The influence of buyers' groups is greater if:

- they are large customers (in volume or spend)
- many substitute products exist
- profit margins are low
- buyers decide to manufacture their own supplies and thereby replace the supplier (backward integration).

Substitutes
The number of perceived substitutes deters existing firms from increasing prices and profits.

Suppliers
Supplier groups are powerful if:

- they are well integrated (for example, a cartel)
- they supply small customers
- their group products are differentiated
- they integrate forward (for example, by setting up their own buyer organizations to replace firms already in the market).

Competition
Competitive rivalry may increase where one or more of the competitors is under threat – for example, from a price war, high exit barriers or economic recession.

Applications

Strategy development
This model could be used to develop a strategy to counter competitive forces.

Positioning
Ideally a firm would aim for a position in which it could counter potential competitive forces. It might also attempt to influence those forces in order to strengthen its position – for example, by improving customer loyalty to deter new entrants.

Enhancing competitive advantage
The model could be applied in anticipating and exploiting changes in the forces ahead of competitors – for example, in the development of a product to counter the effect of an expected substitute.

Related models

- **Ansoff's Box** (see pp. 197–9)
- **Barriers and profitability** (see pp. 47–50)
- **Company position/industry attractiveness screen** (see pp. 137–40)
- **Elasticity** (see pp. 25–8)
- **Five Ps for strategy** (see pp. 65–8)
- **Four routes to strategic advantage** (see pp. 69–72)
- **Generic strategies** (see pp. 73–6)
- **Geobusiness model** (see pp. 77–81)
- **Integrated model of strategic management** (see pp. 155–9)

- **Nine specimen standardized strategies** (see pp. 201–5)
- **PESTLIED** (see pp. 83–6)
- **Porter's Diamond** (see pp. 87–90)
- **Product life cycle** (see pp. 211–14)
- **Strategic triangle** (see pp. 95–8)

Main references

M.E. Porter (1980), *Competitive Strategy: Techniques for Analyzing Industries and Competitors*, New York: The Free Press.
M.E. Porter (1985), *Competitive Advantage: Creating and Sustaining Superior Performance*, New York: The Free Press.

13 Five Ps for strategy

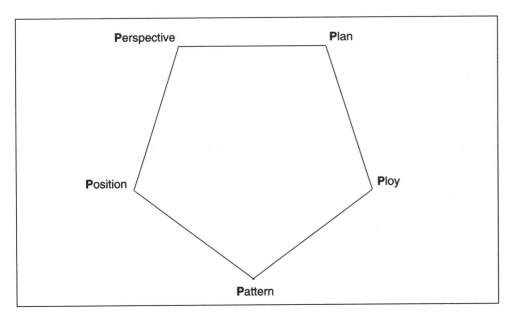

Principle

There is no single definition of strategy; it is possible to consider and define strategy in different ways.

Assumption

Strategy is implemented in many different ways, often depending on the specific requirements at the time – for example, defining activities or products or considering broad market positioning.

Elements

Plan
The Plan is a consciously defined course of action showing how leaders try to establish direction for the organisation.

Ploy
The Ploy is a specific manoeuvre intended to directly outwit a competitor.

Pattern
A Pattern is a consistent, intentional or unintentional pattern of behaviour within a stream of actions.

Position
The Position is a means of defining an organization in relation to its competitive environment.

Perspective
The Perspective is the concept or character of an organization – its collective mind, intention or behaviour.

Issues

Understanding
The five Ps are simply labels to help develop appropriate strategic thinking. They should not define or restrict our thinking but should act as an aid to unravel the complexity implicit in strategy.

Compatibility
The 5P approaches are not mutually exclusive. For example, Position and Perspective should be compatible with Plan and Pattern.

Flexibility
Plans, Positions and Ploys may be easily changed whereas Perspectives and Patterns are longer term and more fundamental.

Programme
A sixth 'P' Programme, – an iterative process that aids progress towards achievement of a vision – might be added.

Applications

As a definition and as an aid to strategy formulation
The term 'strategy' is sometimes ill-used. Use of the five definitions helps to prevent confusion and aids strategy formulation.

As a stimulus to lateral thinking
Consciously considering strategy in different ways can help people to think laterally and creatively about a broad range of issues.

Assessment of strategy
The definitions can be used to analyse the breadth of strategic issues faced by an organization and to help assess strategy from different viewpoints.

Appreciation of strategy issues
The model can help to define both the formal and informal issues impacting on strategy and its development.

Related models

- **Company position/industry attractiveness screen** (see pp. 137–40)
- **Contrasting characteristics of upstream and downstream companies** (see pp. 55–8)
- **Dynamics of paradigm change** (see pp. 145–8)
- **Five forces** (see pp. 59–63)
- **Four routes to strategic advantage** (see pp. 69–72)
- **Organic versus mechanistic management styles** (see pp. 169–72)
- **Patterns of strategic change** (see pp. 173–6)
- **The seven 'S's framework** (see pp. 181–5)

Main reference

H. Mintzberg and J.B. Quinn (1991), *The Strategy Process*, Englewood Cliffs, N.J.: Prentice Hall.

14 Four routes to strategic advantage

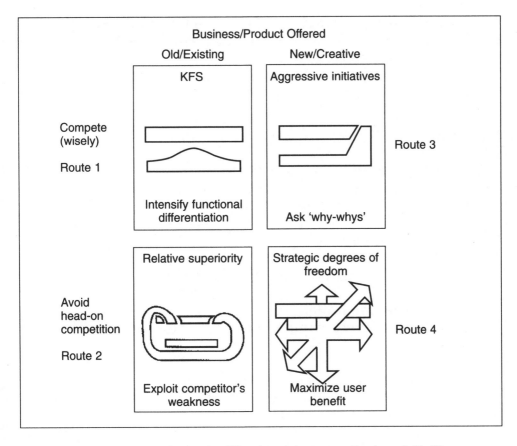

Source: *The Mind of the Strategist (The Art of Japanese Business)*, K. Ohmae, McGraw-Hill, Maidenhead, 1982. Reproduced with the permission of the McGraw-Hill Companies.

Principle

Improved strategic advantage is a function of the nature of the business or product offered and the way in which the organization seeks to compete.

Assumptions

A firm would often perform better if it focused its efforts on improving technological and organizational strengths and satisfying customers rather than on beating competitors.

Strategic planning should be carried out by operational, not just top, management.

Elements

Route 1: key factors for success (KFS)
Resources are allocated where they will be most effective in relation to the identified key success factors.

Route 2: relative superiority
Competitors' weaknesses are exploited using new technology or other strengths, such as an effective sales force.

Route 3: aggressive initiatives
These include direct competition with new business or new products.

Route 4: strategic degrees of freedom
These embrace innovations in products or markets where no competition exists.

Issues

Route 1: KFS
An effective short-cut to success is to concentrate principal resources early within a single strategically significant organizational function.

Route 2: relative superiority
A company may exploit any difference in competitive conditions by analysing competitors' products in detail to determine where it might gain price or cost advantage.

Route 3: aggressive initiatives
This is an unconventional strategy that analyses in detail the established assumptions of an industry or an organization in order to change the direction of strategic thinking. This is how Just-in-Time (JIT) production was created.

Route 4: strategic degrees of freedom
Innovation in products or markets where advantage may be gained can be achieved by first determining the extent and scope of potential changes that might maximize customer satisfaction.

Applications

Strategy formulation
Assessment of KFS and organizational functions assists strategy formulation – for example, in relation to resource allocation.

Product portfolio planning
The model aids product portfolio planning where customer expectations are paramount.

Analysis of strengths and weaknesses
Organizations may use this model to dissect the market

imaginatively in order to identify key segments, discover the particular strengths of winning companies, and analyse differences from losing companies.

Related models

- **Five forces** (see pp. 59–63)
- **Five Ps for strategy** (see pp. 65–8)
- **Generic strategies** (see pp. 73–6)
- **Integrated model of strategic management** (see pp. 155–9)
- **Nine specimen standardized strategies** (see pp. 201–5)
- **Organic versus mechanistic management styles** (see pp. 169–72)
- **Patterns of strategic change** (see pp. 173–6)
- **PIMS competitive strategy paradigm** (see pp. 207–10)
- **Porter's Diamond** (see pp. 87–90)
- **Strategic triangle** (see pp. 95–8)
- **SWOT analysis** (see pp. 187–90)

Main reference

K. Ohmae (1982), *The Mind of the Strategist (The Art of Japanese Business)*, New York: McGraw-Hill.

15 Generic strategies

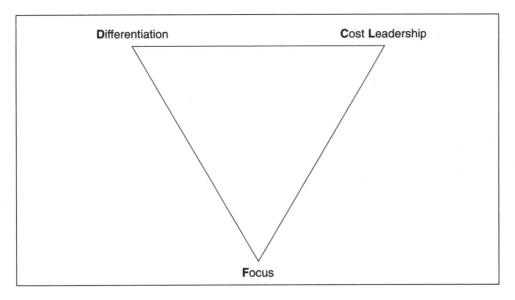

Differentiation   Cost Leadership

Focus

Principle

An organization should identify a strategic direction which is fundamental to establishing and maintaining a strong competitive position.

Assumptions

The organization has sufficient control to be able to make fundamental choices about its strategic direction.

The organization also wishes to grow continuously in a changing and uncertain environment.

Elements

Cost leadership
The firm's strategy is to minimize costs, giving greater flexibility over pricing decisions.

Differentiation
The firm offers a product or service which is different in some way that is valued by customers – for example, through product features or high quality service.

Focus
The organization targets products or services in a particular market sector or market segment.

Issues

Prices
Cost leadership firms may offer average or just below average prices in the industry or market, thereby remaining competitive and gaining high margins.

Flexibility
Cost leadership firms can better cope with cost increases from suppliers and are well placed to combat entry barriers because of economies of scale.

Development
Cost leadership may be gained as organizations become more experienced than competitors in technical, process and marketing activities.

Cost leadership risks
These include obsolescence (for example, retaining old technology), and new entrants to the market copying the leading organization's processes.

Margins
Differentiation can yield higher margins with which to offset the power of suppliers, and also reduces the threat posed by substitutes once customer loyalty is achieved.

Differentiation risks
The cost of remaining differentiated may push prices too high even for loyal customers. As industries mature, imitations which reduce the perceived differentiation may come on to the market.

Focus niche strategy
This strategy has the elements of cost leadership or of differentiation, but relates to a particular market segment.

Focus risks
The organization may become short-sighted and fail to perceive a broader market opportunity or, equally, concentrate too heavily on a volatile market. However, without a generic strategy, the organization may unwittingly seek to be 'all things to all people', and become 'stuck in the middle'.

Applications

Cost leadership
Achieving cost leadership includes setting up and implementing an

effective cost structure, competitive pricing and achieving economies of scale.

Differentiation
Differentiation involves the development of unique product characteristics, improved branding and increased customer loyalty.

Focus
A focus strategy helps to determine the specific competitive advantage that may be gained within a particular market segment.

Related models

- **Contrasting characteristics of upstream and downstream companies** (see pp. 55–8)
- **Five forces** (see pp. 59–63)
- **Four routes to strategic advantage** (see pp. 69–72)
- **Nine specimen standardized strategies** (see pp. 201–5)
- **Porter's Diamond** (see pp. 87–90)
- **Strategic triangle** (see pp. 95–8)
- **SWOT analysis** (see pp. 187–90)

Main references

M.E. Porter (1985), *Competitive Advantage: Creating and Sustaining Superior Performance*, New York: The Free Press.
M.E. Porter (1980), *Competitive Strategy: Techniques for Analyzing Industries and Competitors*, New York: The Free Press.

16 Geobusiness model

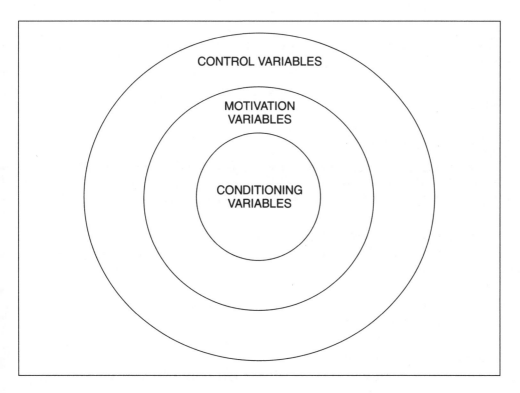

Source: *International Business and Multinational Enterprise*, Robock and Simmonds, Richard D. Irwin Inc, 1989.

Principle

There is a comprehensive framework for explaining and predicting international business patterns.

Assumptions

There are three main interacting forces that affect firms' international business actions.

Elements

Conditioning variables

- **Product-specific variables**: conferring competitive advantages for the foreign investor – for example, R & D, product differentiation, product processing, management skills, know-how, economies of scale
- **Country-specific characteristics**: helping to sustain competitive advantages of firms – for example, economic size of home market, nature of domestic competition, resource scarcity or surplus
- **Inter-nation variables**: for example, tariffs, strategic alliances, international finance.

Motivation variables

This category of variables is concerned with competitive strategy.

- **Market-seeking measures**: horizontal/forward integration
- **Resource-seeking measures**: vertical/backward integration
- **Production efficiency-seeking measures**: for example, lower resource costs
- **Technology-seeking measures**: securing access to foreign technology or skilled labour
- **Risk avoidance measures**: for example, minimising possibilities

of production interruption, improving market control
- **Exchange-of-threat measures**: waging a counter-offensive strategy to disarm a competitor, especially in their home market

Control variables
These comprise administrative actions – that is, laws and policies of home and host governments that directly or indirectly influence international business through positive incentives and/or negative controls.

Issues

International relevance
The model applies to the international business actions of all firms, not just those classified as multinationals.

Effect on organizations
The variables will impact in different ways, depending on the organization's specific activities.

Interdependence
The variables are interlinked – for example, wage-controlled, low labour costs in a particular country may be classified as a country-specific variable (conditioning) and a production-efficiency seeking measure (motivation). Wage control would also be a control variable.

Influence on variables
The organization perceives the conditioning variables (opportunities for competitive advantage), responds appropriately (motivation variables–competitive strategy) but has no influence over control variables.

Applications

Growth strategies
The model may be used in the assessment and development of international business growth strategies.

Growth potential assessment
Another application lies in the assessment of the potential for growth given a change in international conditions – for example, cessation of hostilities or a relaxation of frontier controls such as that which took place in the European Union.

Evaluation
The model can help in the evaluation of international competitors and markets.

Decision-making
The model is an aid in deciding whether or not to embark upon international business activities.

Assessment
The model may be used to assess the relative importance and interaction of the different variables to the organization.

Related models

- **Economies of scale** (see pp. 21–4)
- **Five forces** (see pp. 59–63)
- **Integrated model of strategic management** (see pp. 155–9)
- **Nine specimen standardized strategies** (see pp. 201–5)
- **PESTLIED** (see pp. 83–6)
- **SWOT analysis** (see pp. 187–90)

Main reference

Robock and Simmonds, (1989), *International Business and Multinational Enterprise*, Richard D. Irwin Inc.

17   PESTLIED

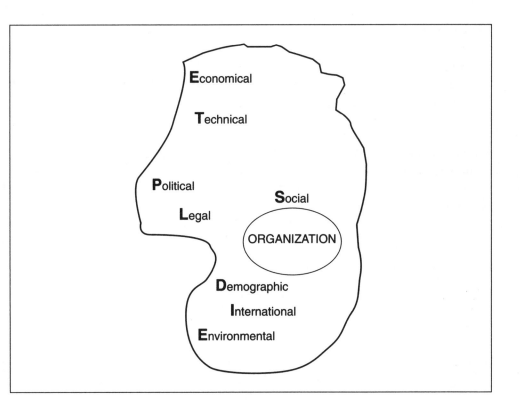

Principle

PESTLIED is a mnemonic which represents various environmental factors that can usefully be addressed when analysing an organization.

Assumption

Various factors in the environment can have a significant impact on the performance of organizations operating within their sphere of influence.

Elements

Political
These factors include local and national government actions that may affect the organization.

Economic
Fiscal policies – for example, interest rates and taxation – may affect the organization.

Social
These factors comprise social trends and tolerance towards the organization and its products.

Technological
These factors include, for example, technological changes that affect demand for products or which impact on the organization's activities.

Legal matters
Legislation, such as that of the European Union, may affect the organization and can inhibit or enhance its performance.

International
These factors include, for example, exchange rates which can influence profitability.

Environmental
These factors are environmental constraints on factory operation,

such as 'green issues'.

Demographic
Demographic factors comprise the availability of workforce, and age differences, which impinge upon organizational performance.

Issues

Negative and positive factors
Several PESTLIED factors may interact negatively or positively. For example, an organization may be welcomed into a new locality (social environment) but may be hampered by adverse government funding arrangements (political/economic environment). In this case, it may be that local unemployment is high but that government initiatives for encouraging organizations to move into the area are not yet in place.

Relative importance of factors
The importance of the various PESTLIED factors varies according to the nature of the organization. For example, to a software house, technical innovation might be expected to be of far greater importance than the social environment.

Other factors
Besides PESTLIED factors, there are other factors or environments that affect organizations – for example, the competitive environment.

Other analysis tools
The PESTLIED analysis tool would usually be employed in conjunction with SWOT (Strengths, Weaknesses, Opportunities, Threats) analysis.

Applications

Analysis and audit
PESTLIED may be used in the analysis and audit of organizations.

Planning
The model may be used as a checklist in the planning process to ensure that the forecast effects of PESTLIED factors are taken into account.

Management development
The use of the list of PESTLIED factors encourages managers to become less insular and to consider the impact of external influences upon their organizations.

Related models

- **Company position/industry attractiveness screen** (see pp. 137–40)
- **Five forces** (see pp. 59–63)
- **Geobusiness model** (see pp. 77–81)
- **Integrated model of strategic management** (see pp. 155–9)
- **Nine specimen standardized strategies** (see pp. 201–5)
- **PIMS competitive strategy paradigm** (see pp. 207–10)
- **Porter's Diamond** (see pp. 87–90)
- **Product life cycle** (see pp. 211–14)
- **Related diversification grid** (see pp. 91–3)
- **SWOT analysis** (see pp. 187–90)

Main reference

Not known.

18 Porter's Diamond

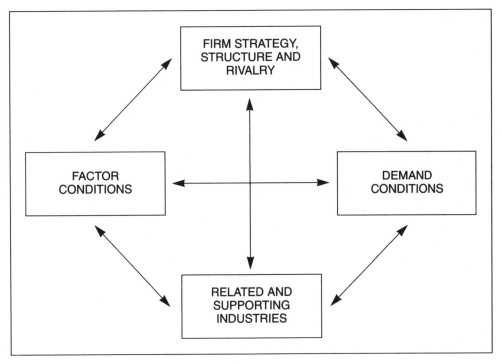

Reproduced from *The Competitive Advantage of Nations* by Michael Porter, London: Macmillan, 1990, with the permission of Macmillan Press Ltd.

Principle

The model shows how a nation's international success within a specified industry depends upon four specific attributes which promote or impede competitive advantage.

Assumption

The competitive environment of an industry within which organizations operate is influenced by four attributes which determine the competitive advantage of the nation for that industry.

Elements

Factor conditions
Factor conditions are the state of the nation's factors of production, such as labour, land, capital, natural resources and infrastructure.

Demand conditions
Demand conditions are the nature and extent of demand within the nation for the industry's services and products.

Related and supporting industries
The presence or absence of related and supporting industries that are internationally competitive is a third attribute in the model.

Strategy, structure, rivalry
Firms' strategy, structure and rivalry describes how organizations are created, managed and compete within the industry.

Issues

Competitive environment
The four attributes interact to create the competitive environment in which the organizations operate.

Relationships between attributes
Increases in one attribute can stimulate other attributes. For example, an improvement in organizational strategy and structure will usually lead to improvements in demand and in supply or utilization of factors of production.

Prosperity
Organizations prosper particularly with access to specialized assets and skills, best information, effective management, investment and innovation.

Reasons for failure
Even when the four attributes are strong some organizations fail because they either do not take advantage of opportunities or they possess relatively low levels of skills and resources.

Further attributes
Two further attributes can influence national competitive advantage: chance events outside an organization's control (such as technological innovation), and government actions (such as investment and taxation).

Industry clusters
Nations succeed not in individual industries but in clusters of industries whose performance reflects the state of the national economy.

Applications

Audit
The model may be applied to individual industries, organizations or business units in order to audit strength of the four attributes and so assess competitive advantage.

Strategy review
Strategy may be reviewed to improve utilization of factors of production and so contribute towards improving competitive advantage of the organization or business unit.

Strategic alliances
Understanding of the model can encourage the formation of

strategic alliances between organizations to improve the state of 'related and supporting industries'.

Related models

- **Company position/industry attractiveness screen** (see pp. 137–40)
- **Elasticity** (see pp. 25–8)
- **Five forces** (see pp. 59–63)
- **Four routes to strategic advantage** (see pp. 69–72)
- **Generic strategies** (see pp. 73–6)
- **M-O-S-T** (see pp. 161–3)
- **Nine specimen standardized strategies** (see pp. 201–5)
- **PESTLIED** (see pp. 83–6)
- **PIMS competitive strategy paradigm** (see pp. 207–10)
- **Strategic triangle** (see pp. 95–8)

Main reference

Michael E. Porter (1990), *The Competitive Advantage of Nations*, London: Macmillan Press.

19 Related diversification grid

Industry attractiveness	Business position		
	High	Medium	Low
High	No diversification	R–CD	R–CD
Medium	R–SD	No diversification	R–CD
Low	R–SD	R–SD	No diversification

Key R–CD = Related–complementary diversification
R–SD = Related–supplementary diversification

Adapted with the permission of The Free Press, a division of Simon & Schuster from *DIVERSIFICATION THROUGH ACQUISITION: Strategies for creating economic value* by Malcolm S. Salter and Wolf A. Weinhold. Copyright © 1979 by Malcolm S. Salter and Wolf A. Weinhold.

Principle

An organization considering 'related' diversification through acquisition should appraise the target company's strengths within its particular industry sector.

Assumption

The degree of compatibility of critical success factors between an organization and a target acquisition will significantly affect the success of the acquisition.

Elements

Related–supplementary diversification (R–SD)
This occurs when a company expands by entering product markets that call for functional skills identical to those it already possesses. An example might be a car engine manufacturer diversifying into other engine types such as marine engines, or acquiring a similar company in a different geographical region.

Related–complementary diversification (R–CD)
This occurs when a company adds key functional activities and skills to those it already has, but does not substantially change its final product market. An example of R–CD is backward integration.

Issues

Purpose of acquisition
The purpose of the acquisition should be evaluated and clearly defined before going ahead.

Related acquisitions
Related acquisitions are normally less problematic than unrelated acquisitions, but the degree and area of relationship are critical.

Compatibility
A good fit with respect to culture, management style and cash flow between the company and the target acquisition is essential if the acquisition is to succeed.

Related diversification and synergy
Related diversification can result in lower unit costs and improved margins through synergy.

Applications

Strategy development
The model may assist with the development of strategic actions designed to overcome weaknesses and/or capitalize on strengths in the parent company through acquisition.

Targeting acquisitions
The model may help with the identification of candidate acquisitions with high potential through an analysis of acquiring company strengths.

Portfolio analysis
Analysis of the portfolio of business units of a diversified company is facilitated by the model.

Related models

- **Company position/industry attractiveness screen** (see pp. 137–40)
- **Cultural web** (see pp. 141–4)
- **PESTLIED** (see pp. 83–86)
- **PIMS competitive strategy paradigm** (see pp. 207–10)
- **The seven 'S's framework** (see pp. 181–5)

Main reference

M.S. Salter and W.A. Weinhold (1979), *Diversification through Acquisition: Strategies for Creating Economic Value*, New York: The Free Press.

20 Strategic triangle

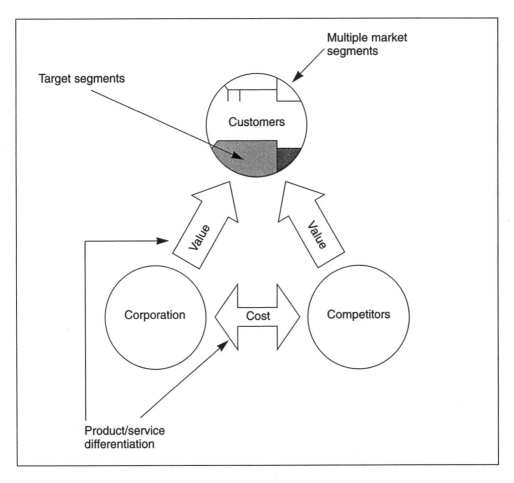

Source: *The Mind of the Strategist (The Art of Japanese Business)*, K. Ohmae, McGraw-Hill, Maidenhead, 1982. Reproduced with the permission of the McGraw-Hill Companies.

Principle

There are three main interest groups in the development of any business strategy.

Assumptions

Each of the three Cs (customers, competitors, corporation) has its own interests which interact.

The role of the strategist is to achieve superior performance relative to competitors whilst ensuring the strategy is consistent with the strengths of the organization and needs of the market.

Strategic planning should be carried out by operational, not just top, management.

Elements

Customers
These are the customers inside as well as outside the organization.

Corporation
This encompasses all the organization's functional units and processes.

Competitors
These are the external and internal competing stakeholders.

Value
This is the benefit added to customers from the corporation and competitors in terms of, for example quality, service and price.

Cost
The relative costs of production between a corporation and its competitors, which may differentiate the product/service.

Issues

Performance
Superior performance can be achieved by an organization differentiating itself from its competitors using its relative corporate strengths to better satisfy customer needs.

Choice of strategists
Strategists are best placed where they are able to deal with all of the organization's key customer segments, all key functions of the corporation and all the key aspects of competitors.

Choice of strategists
Different strategists may result from focusing on different points of the strategic triangle: customers, corporation and competitors.

Applications

Developing customer-based strategies
The market is segmented, and changes to product applications, customer mix and other product attributes may be engineered using this model, to satisfy customer trends.

Developing corporate-based strategies
The model may be used to identify, select and sequence key functions in order to optimize, for example, make-or-buy decisions, or improve functional performance or cost-effectiveness.

Developing competitor-based strategies
Differences between the company and its competitors are linked to one or more of the elements which determine profit: price, volume or cost. Thus, a strategy for achieving a higher price through a differentiated product may lead to better profit performance. A powerful image may be reflected in a price premium.

Functional analysis
The model may be used to analyse the interaction of different functional units within an organization.

Assessment of strengths and weaknesses
The model may be applied to assess the organization's activities – for example, in relation to competitors, customer focus and product portfolio – and to evaluate the profit contribution of different functional units.

Related models

- **Economies of scale** (see pp. 21–4)
- **Five forces** (see pp. 59–63)
- **Four routes to strategic advantage** (see pp. 69–72)
- **Generic strategies** (see pp. 73–6)
- **M-O-S-T** (see pp. 161–3)
- **Nine specimen standardized strategies** (see pp. 201–5)
- **PIMs competitive strategy paradigm** (see pp. 207–10)
- **Porter's Diamond** (see pp. 87–90)
- **The seven 'S's framework** (see pp. 181–5)
- **SWOT analysis** (see pp. 187–90)

Main reference

K. Ohmae (1982), *The Mind of the Strategist (The Art of Japanese Business)*, New York: McGraw-Hill.

Human resources

21 Action-centred leadership

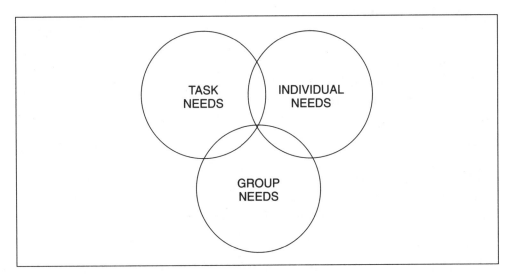

Source: *Effective Leadership*, John Adair, Gower, Aldershot, 1983.

Principle

When leading a group of people, it is important for the leaders to consider task needs, individual needs and group maintenance needs.

Assumption

Although they overlap, group, individual and task needs are distinct.

Elements

Task needs
These include defining the task, planning, allocating resources and controlling and monitoring progress.

Individual needs
These include development, motivation and recognition of people.

Group needs
These include team building, communication, coordination, setting standards and managing conflict.

Issues

Balanced leadership
A good leader is able to move between the three elements effectively, achieving a balanced approach.

Harmony
The degree of overlap of the circles in the model represents the degree to which the elements are in harmony.

Focus
In particular circumstances, it may be necessary to give concentrated attention to one element. For example, a crisis will normally demand more focus on the task. Alternatively, when forming a group, team needs may be most important.

Tension
It is important to distinguish the individual from the group, to be aware of potential tension and to manage it.

Applications

Encouraging balanced leadership
Appreciation of the model's principles helps the manager to consider and encourage balanced leadership.

Appraisal
The model's elements may be used to assess the effectiveness of managers and leaders. They may also be employed when appraising staff in relation to their ability to perform a task and work with others.

Relevance at all organizational levels
The model may be applied at levels other than the primary, team level – for example, at organizational or business unit levels.

Related models

- **Belbin's team roles** (see pp. 105–8)
- **Cultural web** (see pp. 141–4)
- **Herzberg's Motivator–Hygiene Theory** (see pp. 113–15)
- **Job characteristics** (see pp. 117–20)
- **Maslow's hierarchy of needs** (see pp. 125–9)
- **Situational leadership** (see pp. 131–4)

Main reference

J. Adair (1983), *Effective Leadership*, Aldershot: Gower.

22 Belbin's team roles

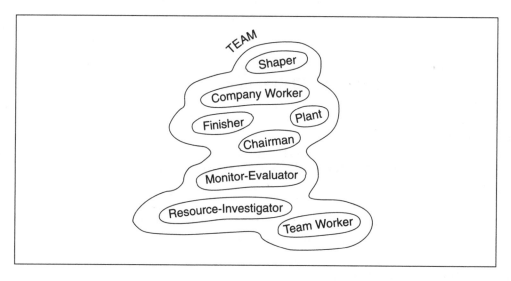

Source: *Management Teams: Why they succeed or fail*, R.M. Belbin Butterworth-Heinemann, Oxford, 1984.

Principle

There are eight roles that interact to form a fully effective team.

Assumption

Roles played by team members are critical to the effectiveness of team performance.

Elements

There are eight roles.

Chairman
This individual is the disciplined, focused, balanced coordinator. He or she is a good listener and works through others.

Shaper
This team member is highly strung, outgoing and dominant. He or she acts as a passionate catalyst of action, but can be irritable and impatient.

Plant
The Plant is introverted but intellectually dominant. Imaginative, with original ideas, he or she hates detail and resents criticism.

Monitor-Evaluator
This is the analytical thinker, who provides a quality check. He or she is dependable but can be tactless and cold.

Resource-Investigator
This team member develops new contacts and ideas. The Resource-investigator is popular, extroverted, sociable and relaxed but is not an original thinker or a driver.

Company Worker
This is the practical organizer who turns ideas into action through scheduling and planning. He or she is unexciting but a good administrator.

Team Worker
The Team Worker holds the team together by supporting, listening, harmonizing and understanding. Unexciting but essential.

Finisher
The Finisher helps the team meet the deadlines and drives others along, possibly to their annoyance.

Issues

Rapid change
All eight roles are required to introduce and manage rapid change, most effectively.

Number of roles
Stable groups could perform effectively with fewer roles. In a small team one member may have to perform more than one role, and managers consistently tend to adopt one or two team roles.

Formal status
Team roles are not necessarily associated with an individual's formal status. For example, the senior manager may not be a natural Chairman or Shaper and might be more effectively used within his or her 'natural' role.

Personal agendas
Regardless of their roles, team members may bring personal agendas to the team which may limit effective performance towards common group goals.

Times of crisis
The importance and interaction of the roles increases during times of crisis and emergency, improving team cohesion.

Mature groups
As groups mature and their activities change, the importance of different roles varies.

Own best role
It is possible to predict an individual's 'natural' role using

psychometric testing. Self-awareness and selecting one's own best role enhances performance within that role.

Applications

Assessment
Assessing the effectiveness of teams, individuals' roles and contributions to a team.

Team development
Developing existing teams and forming teams for a particular task.

Task assignment
Assigning tasks to existing teams.

Predicting team conflicts
The model may be used when assessing the possible bases for conflict in a team.

Related models

- **Action-centred leadership** (see pp. 101–3)
- **Cultural web** (see pp. 141–4)
- **Four organizational cultures** (see pp. 149–53)
- **Group development** (see pp. 109–12)
- **Herzberg's Motivator–Hygiene Theory** (see pp. 113–15)
- **Maslow's hierarchy of needs** (see pp. 125–9)
- **Resource allocation at corporate level** (see pp. 177–80)
- **The seven 'S's framework** (see pp. 181–5)

Main reference

R.M. Belbin (1984), *Management Teams: Why they Succeed or Fail*, Oxford: Butterworth-Heinemann.

23   Group development

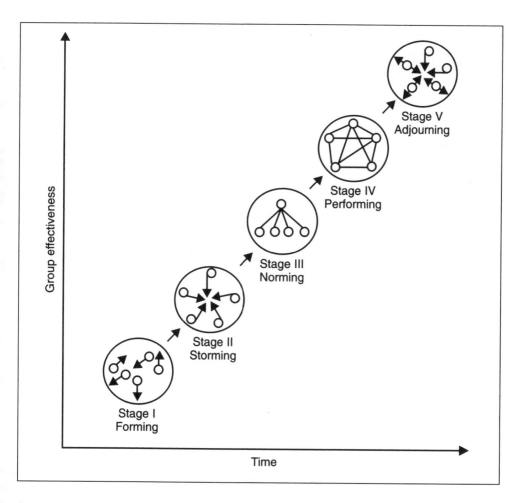

Source: 'Stages of Small Group Development Revisited' by B. Tuckman and N. Jensen in *Group and Organisational Studies*, **2**, 109 1977.

Principle

Groups mature and develop through five stages of growth: forming, storming, norming, performing and adjourning.

Assumption

Teams and groups manifest different identifiable states depending on their development over time.

Elements

Forming
In forming stage, individual group members get to know one another.

Storming
This is an uncomfortable, conflictual stage. Different individual needs may clash both with others' and group needs.

Norming
In this stage working rules are established and roles are allocated.

Performing
The mature group carries out its task effectively.

Adjourning
The group may disband because their job is done or because members are leaving.

Issues

Formation of groups
A group forms either naturally, by means of sharing a common

purpose or interest, or it may be formed artificially for a particular task.

Selection of group members
For an artificially formed group, members must be carefully selected, taking account of both the purpose of the group and the personal attributes of the members.

Selection by leaders
Leaders may tend to select members who are similar in some way to themselves, rather than those who can contribute most effectively to the task.

Interaction of group members
As relative positions are established, the group develops 'norms' or unwritten informal rules which govern the way members interact and lay down acceptable behaviours for the future. Once basic norms have been developed the group can perform effectively.

Disbanding the group
As the life of the group comes to an end and members part company, it may be necessary to help members through this transition by having 'ceremonies', such as farewell parties or other social rituals.

Experiencing the five stages
Groups should be given the space to go through, and not attempt to bypass, the five different stages within the model.

Leadership styles
An effective group leader will recognize the dynamics at each stage and adapt his or her leadership style to the needs of individuals and the group whilst carrying out the task.

Applications

Understanding behaviours
The model helps leaders and group members to develop an understanding of their different personal attitudes and behaviours as a group develops.

Development of leadership styles
The model helps leaders consider the most appropriate leadership styles for different stages in group development.

Management of change
The model is an aid to understanding and managing both general organizational change and group changes.

Related models

- **Action-centred leadership** (see pp. 89–91)
- **Belbin's team roles** (see pp. 105–8)
- **Cultural web** (see pp. 141–4)
- **Four organizational cultures** (see pp. 149–53)
- **Job characteristics** (see pp. 117–20)
- **Maslow's hierarchy of needs** (see pp. 125–9)
- **Situational leadership** (see pp. 131–4)

Main references

B. Tuckman and N. Jensen (1977), 'Stages of Small Group Development Revisited', *Group and Organisational Studies*, **2**.

A. Huczynski and D. Buchanan (1991), *Organizational Behaviour*, Englewood Cliffs, N.J.: Prentice Hall.

24 Herzberg's Motivator–Hygiene Theory

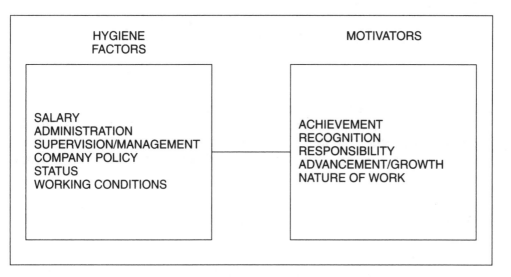

HYGIENE FACTORS	MOTIVATORS
SALARY	ACHIEVEMENT
ADMINISTRATION	RECOGNITION
SUPERVISION/MANAGEMENT	RESPONSIBILITY
COMPANY POLICY	ADVANCEMENT/GROWTH
STATUS	NATURE OF WORK
WORKING CONDITIONS	

Adapted from exhibit 9, 'Factors Affecting Job Attitudes as Reported in 12 Investigations', in Frederick Herzberg's 'One more time: how do you motivate employees?', *Harvard Business Review*, September/October, 1987.

Principle

There are two principal classes of needs that affect satisfaction and motivation – satisfiers/motivators and hygiene factors.

Assumption

Factors which lead to work satisfaction are fundamentally different in nature to those which lead to dissatisfaction.

Elements

Hygiene factors or context factors
These factors do not positively motivate when they are present but demotivate when they are absent. They include salary, administration, supervision and management, company policy, status and working conditions.

Satisfiers/motivators or content factors
These factors can positively motivate when present in work and demotivate when absent. They include achievement, recognition, responsibility, advancement and growth and the nature of the work itself.

Issues

Job enrichment
From this theory, Herzberg developed the notion of job-enrichment – that is, increasing people's satisfaction and motivation by increasing the 'motivators' or 'content factors'.

Individual responses
People are different and do not respond to different factors to the same degree – for example, achievement will vary in the extent to which it motivates. It is not true that the more motivators that are contained in a job, the more it will motivate. The potential to motivate depends on the needs, interests and attributes of individuals. More recent research has suggested that this is not a theory for Western societies only, but is universal across different cultures.

Importance of hygiene factors

Hygiene factors should be improved in order to reduce dissatisfaction as a first step in improving work. Motivators may not be effective until these are satisfactory.

Applications

Work design

The model may be used to assess current work designs to determine dissatisfying elements and to decide where dissatisfiers can be removed. Consideration may then be given to how work and work methods might be redesigned to increase motivation and benefit the organization.

Assessment of individuals

The model may be used when considering individual differences in motivation and job design, and in matching individuals to jobs.

Related models

- **Action-centred leadership** (see pp. 101–3)
- **Belbin's team roles** (see pp. 105–8)
- **Cultural web** (see pp. 141–4)
- **Job characteristics** (see pp. 117–20)
- **Maslow's heirarchy of needs** (see pp. 125–9)
- **Situational leadership** (see pp. 131–4)

Main reference

F. Herzberg (1968), 'One more time: how do you motivate employees?', *Harvard Business Review*, **46**, pp. 53–62.

25 Job characteristics

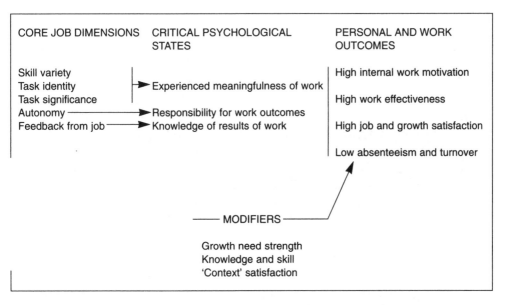

CORE JOB DIMENSIONS   CRITICAL PSYCHOLOGICAL   PERSONAL AND WORK
STATES   OUTCOMES

Skill variety   High internal work motivation
Task identity   Experienced meaningfulness of work
Task significance   High work effectiveness
Autonomy   Responsibility for work outcomes
Feedback from job   Knowledge of results of work   High job and growth satisfaction

Low absenteeism and turnover

—— MODIFIERS ——

Growth need strength
Knowledge and skill
'Context' satisfaction

Principle

The Model shows the link between dimensions of jobs, the experience of people in the job and the psychological and behavioural outcomes that may be expected.

Assumptions

People differ with respect to the elements that motivate them and the degree to which they are motivated by a job. Certain elements in a job increase its potential to motivate job-holders but positive outcomes for them depend primarily on a good match between the job and job-holder.

Elements

Core job dimensions

- **Skill variety**: the use of different skills and competencies
- **Task identity**: carrying out a meaningful piece of work
- **Task significance**: the effect the task has on others
- **Autonomy**: individual freedom, discretion and independence
- **Feedback**: having knowledge of the results of the work, from doing the job itself and from others
- **Dealing with others**: interacting, developing relationships and progressing the work with other people

Critical psychological states

- **Meaningfulness**: carrying out something which is worthwhile
- **Responsibility**: degree of accountability for work outcomes
- **Knowledge of results**: understanding how well work is done.

Modifiers

- **Growth need strength**: the degree of need to learn, develop and achieve in work
- **Knowledge and skill**: the degree of job-holder competence
- **Context satisfaction**: the degree to which the work environment is satisfactory

Personal and work outcomes

- Positive outcomes result where there is a good fit between core job dimensions, critical psychological states and modifiers.

Issues

Matching job to job-holder
A job motivates primarily because there is a good match between the job and job holder. Questionnaires have been developed with this model and can be used to assess a job and the job-holder's response to it.

Motivation
Increasing the job dimensions in a job increases its potential to motivate, but a person with a low growth need strength may be more motivated in a job with lower levels of job dimensions.

Psychological states
Motivation depends on experiencing all three of the critical psychological states, not just one or two of them. Positive psychological responses lead to positive outcomes both for the organization and the person.

Modifiers
The relationship between the job dimensions, psychological states and outcomes is affected by the modifiers. If knowledge and skill is not at least adequate, if the work environment (context) is demotivating or if the person has a low growth need strength, then even a job with high levels of the necessary elements may not motivate the job-holder.

Applications

Assessment of current work organization and job design
The model may be used as a basis for redesigning work systems including procedures, task allocation and team working. It may also be used to design management systems involving communication structures, feedback channels, and levels of delegation and responsibility.

Job matching
The model may be applied in matching jobs to job-holders.

Motivation
The model may be employed as a framework to consider the motivation and behaviours of staff.

Non-work activity analysis
A further application is in the consideration of non-work activities.

Related models

- **Action-centred leadership** (see pp. 101–3)
- **Group development** (see pp. 109–12)
- **Herzberg's Motivator – Hygiene Theory** (see pp. 113–15)
- **Managerial grid** (see pp. 121–4)
- **Maslow's hierarchy of needs** (see pp. 125–9)
- **Organic versus mechanistic management styles** (see pp. 169–72)
- **Situational leadership** (see pp. 131–4)

Main reference

J.R. Hackman, G. Oldham, R Janson and K. Purdy (1975), *California Management Review*, **17** (4) p. 62. (reprinted by permission of the Regents of the University of California).

26 Managerial grid®

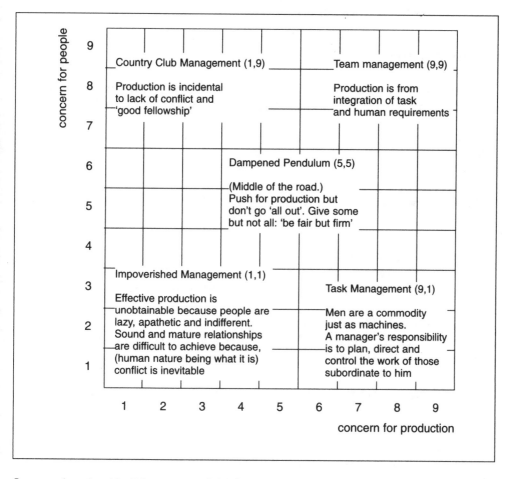

Source: *Leadership Dilemmas – Grid Solutions* by Robert R. Blake and Anne Adams McCanse, Houston: Gulf Publishing Company, page 29. Copyright © 1991 by Scientific Methods, Inc.

Principle

The managerial grid plots a manager's style in terms of concern for people versus concern for production, which can be measured using a diagnostic questionnaire. Although the two concerns can be evaluated independently of one another on the axes, in this model they form a grid and are used interdependently.

Assumptions

People tend towards a natural management style and this style can be classified in terms of its balance between people issues and task issues.

Elements

Concern for people
This is the degree of interest in people's needs, wants, feelings, opinions and other individual attributes.

Concern for production
This is the degree of interest in tasks, resources, structures and procedures that contribute to achievement of work targets.

Country Club Management (1, 9)
In this position, good relations are central but there is minimal concern for the achievement of work results.

Team Management (9, 9)
Here, concern for both people and work issues are very high.

Impoverished management (1, 1)
The manager in this position displays little concern for either people or work activities.

Task Management (9, 1)
In this position, concern for work activities is high but little interest in people is displayed.

Dampened pendulum (5, 5)
Here, concern for both people issues and work issues is 'middle of the road'.

Issues

Style
The managerial grid is based on a one-person/one-style belief, called a dominant approach. Each manager has his or her own grid style which may or may not be applicable in all situations. A particular style may be most appropriate at particular times and in particular circumstances. For example, task management may be the most effective style in a situation where staff have a low desire for independence or during a crisis. On the other hand country club management may be the best approach with a group of experts or self-motivated people. An effective manager is able to adapt his or her style over the grid to suit different circumstances.

Task management style
The task management style (9, 1) may lead to higher productivity in the short term but lower morale and lower productivity in the long term.

Team management style
Although effective management depends on the particular situation, in general, a manager will be most effective in the team management position (9, 9) where task and human requirements are integrated. The team management style works in any situation because co-operation and support makes even the hardest decisions acceptable to the team.

Applications

Appraisal
The model may help in the appraisal of managers.

Development
The model can raise self-awareness of managers as a basis for development.

Matching
The model can help match managers with types of work activity and assist in assigning staff to a particular manager to ensure best fit.

Analysis
The model may be used to analyse organizational styles.

Related models

- **Action-centred leadership** (see pp. 101–3)
- **Cultural web** (see pp. 141–4)
- **Job characteristics** (see pp. 117–20)
- **Maslow's hierarchy of needs** (see pp. 125–9)
- **Situational leadership** (see pp. 131–4)

Main reference

R. Blake and J. Mouton (1964), *The Managerial Grid*, Houston: Gulf.

27 Maslow's hierarchy of needs

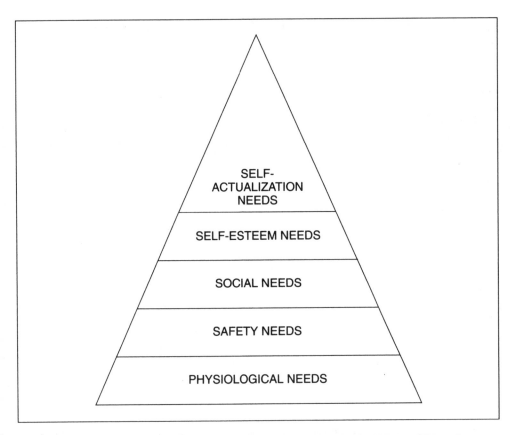

"Maslow's Hierarchy of Needs" from *MOTIVATION AND PERSONALITY*, 3rd Edition by Abraham H. Maslow. Copyright © 1954,1987 by Harper & Row, Publishers, Inc. Copyright © 1970 by Abraham H. Maslow. Reprinted by permission of Addison Wesley Educational Publishers Inc.

Principle

People have different needs which can be grouped and ordered to indicate relative importance.

Assumption

People have similar fundamental need-patterns that they wish to satisfy and they move between different groups of needs in similar ways.

Elements

Hierarchy
A person moves from lower-order needs, with physiological as the most basic, to higher needs as each need level is (generally) satisfied.

Physiological needs
These comprise survival-related needs, such as hunger and thirst.

Safety needs
These comprise security and the absence of threat.

Social needs
These are affiliation and close relationships.

Self-esteem needs
Self-respect and a sense of own value are critical to self-esteem.

Self-actualization needs
These needs comprise the utilization and growth of skills and abilities and also self-fulfilment through achieving potential.

Issues

Nature of the Model
Maslow developed the theory from anecdotal, not empirical, evidence. The model is not intended to be a rigid description of attitudes and behaviour but a typical picture of what can happen in ideal conditions. It is intended to reflect life in general, not just work motivation.

Salient needs
The model suggests that people are motivated by salient needs – that is, needs which are not yet satisfied and which are situated at the next level up on the hierarchy. However, for some people, higher needs have been found to be important even when lower needs have not been satisfied.

Individuals' needs
The model represents individuals' experience. Different people are at different places on the hierarchy and the same person can move up and down the hierarchy depending on their circumstances. Moving between groups of needs can be very rapid following a single change – for example, through redundancy.

Order of need
In most developed societies higher order needs (for example self-esteem) are generally salient. However, with the threat of redundancy and work uncertainty, many people are motivated by safety/security needs. Lower order (survival/security) needs are generally satisfiable – for example, a meal will eliminate the need to eat. However, highe   eds are often not satisfiable – for example, the need   a does not diminish as growth is achieved; in fact, it m   forced.

Applications

Understanding motivation
The model helps managers to understand the different factors that may motivate different people and why people respond differently to possibilities of satisfying different needs.

Understanding how needs change over time
At a time of change, its potential effect on people's position on the hierarchy might be considered. An organization's policies and practices may be redefined to satisfy these changing needs and so remotivate people.

Team building
When developing a team the model may be used to help define the personal profile of aspiring team members and so assist in their selection.

Related models

- **Belbin's team roles** (see pp. 105–8)
- **Group development** (see pp. 109–12)
- **Herzberg's Motivator – Hygiene Theory** (see pp. 113–15)
- **Job characteristics** (see pp. 117–20)
- **Managerial grid** (see pp. 121–4)
- **Organic versus mechanistic management styles** (see pp. 169–72)
- **The seven 'S's framework** (see pp. 181–5)
- **Situational leadership** (see pp. 131–4)

Main references

A. Maslow (1943), 'A Theory of Human Motivation', *Psychological Review*, **50**, (4).

A. Maslow (1987), *Motivation and Personality*, (3rd edn), New York: Harper and Row.

28 Situational leadership

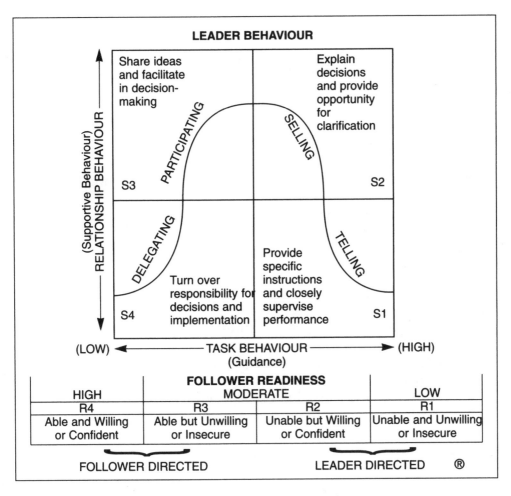

LEADER BEHAVIOUR

(Supportive Behaviour) RELATIONSHIP BEHAVIOUR

S3 PARTICIPATING	S2 SELLING
Share ideas and facilitate in decision-making	Explain decisions and provide opportunity for clarification
S4 DELEGATING	S1 TELLING
Turn over responsibility for decisions and implementation	Provide specific instructions and closely supervise performance

(LOW) ◄── TASK BEHAVIOUR ──► (HIGH)
(Guidance)

FOLLOWER READINESS			
HIGH	MODERATE		LOW
R4	R3	R2	R1
Able and Willing or Confident	Able but Unwilling or Insecure	Unable but Willing or Confident	Unable and Unwilling or Insecure

FOLLOWER DIRECTED   LEADER DIRECTED   ®

Principle

The most effective leadership style depends both on the amount of direction and support given and the readiness of the group to carry out the task.

Assumption

There is no single best style of leadership; the best style depends on the situation.

Elements

Dimensions

- **Task behaviour**: the amount of guidance or direction the leader gives
- **Relationship behaviour**: the amount of social or supportive behaviour employed by the leader

Styles

- **Delegating**: handing over the responsibility for decisions and implementation of tasks to others
- **Participating**: acting as a facilitator through informal support and relationships
- **Selling**: providing guidance on the task but giving opportunity for discussion
- **Telling**: giving clear instructions and closely controlling task activities

Issues

Changing leadership styles
A leader may move from a 'telling' approach to 'delegating' as

people become more competent and ready to take on tasks.

Effective leadership
A person who can move between styles, to suit the situation, would normally be a more effective leader than one who exhibits limited flexibility in style.

Maturity
The movement of people from inability and unwillingness (R1) to ability and willingness (R4) has been associated with their degree of 'maturity'. The more mature the staff, the more likely a participative or delegating style will be appropriate.

Applications

Assessing leadership styles
The model may be used as a framework to assess existing leadership styles. It may also be used to assess a dominant style within an organizational culture – for example, a bureaucratic organization may tend towards a 'telling' style.

Group dimensions
The model may be used to identify the most important dimensions in the relationship between a leader and a group and to consider the most appropriate style for a particular task or for a particular group. It can also be helpful in identifying reasons for problems that may exist between a leader and a group.

Assessment of individuals
The model may be applied to individuals or to groups but, within groups, individual differences in ability, readiness and preferred leadership style must be considered.

Related models

- **Action-centred leadership** (see pp. 101–3)
- **Belbin's team roles** (see pp. 105–8)
- **Cultural web** (see pp. 141–4)
- **Four organizational cultures** (see pp. 149–53)
- **Group development** (see pp. 109–12)
- **Herzberg's Motivator – Hygiene Theory** (see pp. 113–15)
- **Job characteristics** (see pp. 117–20)
- **Managerial grid** (see pp. 121–4)
- **Maslow's heirarchy of needs** (see pp. 125–9)
- **Organic versus mechanistic management styles** (see pp. 169–72)
- **The seven 'S's framework** (see pp. 181–5)

Main references

P. Hersey and K.H. Blanchard (1988), *Management of Organizational Behaviour: Utilizing Human Resources*, Englewood Cliffs, N.J.: Prentice Hall.

A. Huczynski and D. Buchanan (1991), *Organizational Behaviour*, Englewood Cliffs, N.J.: Prentice Hall.

Organizational strategy

29 Company position/industry attractiveness screen

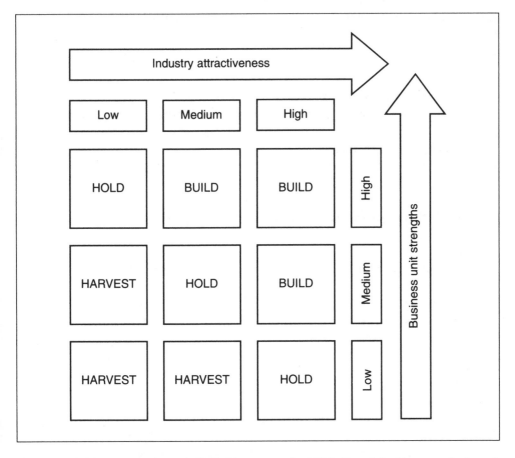

Source: *Making strategy work*, R.G. Hamermesh, 1986. Reprinted by permission of John Wiley & Sons, Inc.

Principle

Portfolio planning can have a significant influence on strategy formulation.

Assumption

Because resources are limited their allocation should be based on a combination of industry attractiveness and the relative strengths of different business units in a diversified organization.

Elements

Industry attractiveness
This includes market growth, size, profitability and price policies.

Business unit strengths
This includes size, market share and technological standing.

Build
Growth through investment is a central objective.

Hold
Investment is maintained and assessed continuously.

Harvest
Remove cash from the business unit and invest elsewhere.

Issues

Business unit definition
Business units should be defined very carefully because definitions shape market perceptions, are influenced by administration and resource considerations and must be responsive to changes in markets, competition and technology.

Negotiations between managers
Portfolio planning tends to centralize the strategic process. If the devolution of strategy setting is an objective, corporate and unit managements must be permitted to negotiate about cash flow and strategic objectives.

Other techniques
Portfolio planning should not be equated with overall strategy; other techniques should also be used.

Applications

Strategy formulation
The model can help in the formulation of organizational and business unit strategy, understanding of markets and the firm's position within them.

Project funding
Portfolio planning is a first step in determining whether a business unit which is proposing a project is worthy of funding at all.

Restructuring
The model may be used to assess an organization's strategic position after a cash crisis in order to effectively divest cash-hungry businesses and promote divestitures and corporate restructuring.

Market planning
Portfolio planning helps in deciding which market to compete in and which resources to use.

Related models

- **Ansoff's Box** (see pp. 197–9)
- **Barriers and profitability** (see pp. 47–50)

- **Company position/industry attractiveness screen** (see pp. 137–40)
- **Contrasting characteristics of upstream and downstream companies** (see pp. 55–8)
- **Five forces** (see pp. 59–63)
- **Five Ps for strategy** (see 65–8)
- **Nine specimen standardized strategies** (see pp. 201–5)
- **PESTLIED** (see pp. 83–6)
- **PIMS competitive strategy paradigm** (see pp. 207–10)
- **Porter's Diamond** (see pp. 87–90)
- **Related diversification grid** (see pp. 91–3)
- **Resource allocation at corporate level** (see pp. 177–80)
- **Value chain** (see pp. 191–4)

Main reference

R.G. Hamermesh (1986), *Making Strategy Work – How Senior Managers Produce Results*, Chichester: John Wiley and Sons.

30 Cultural web

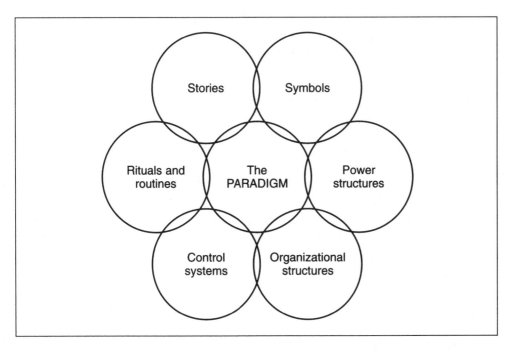

Source: *Exploring Corporate Strategy*, G. Johnson and K. Scholes, Prentice Hall, London, 1993.

Principle

The interaction of key factors influences the way an organization operates (culture).

Assumption

The *paradigm*, which develops from the key factors, is central to the ongoing success of the organization.

Elements

Paradigm/recipe
The paradigm comprises the combined key beliefs and assumptions and is influenced by the following factors:

- **stories**: stories of past achievements, procedural activities
- **symbols**: indications of status – for example titles, office size, job perks
- **rituals and routines**: any well established formal or informal procedures
- **power structures**: traditional power base, promotion rights and expectations
- **control systems**: formal regulation within all functional areas
- **organizational structures**: the formal relationship between the different elements of an organization – for example, functional/centralized/hierarchical.

Issues

Paradigm changes
Lasting strategic change comes about through changes in the paradigm.

Integration
An organization's culture is strongest when all factors are integrated and contribute positively to the paradigm, often giving stability and confidence to the organization and its people.

Weakness
If one of the key factors is very weak – for example, there is a lack of

internal audit controls – the effect on the organization can be catastrophic.

Ease of change
Some factors – for example, symbols and routines – may be more easily changed than others. Some organizations restructure regularly but at great expense and incurring significant disruption in human terms.

Applications

Analysis
- of a whole organization, a business unit or team
- of an industry – for example banking
- of the interaction between factors – for example, how formal controls may be compromised by power structures.

Cultural change
One or more of the factors, or even the paradigm itself, may be changed – for example with the arrival of a new chief executive.

Related models

- **Action-centred leadership** (see pp. 101–3)
- **Belbin's team roles** (see pp. 105–8)
- **Dynamics of paradigm change** (see pp. 145–8)
- **Four organizational cultures** (see pp. 149–53)
- **Group development** (see pp. 109–12)
- **Herzberg's Motivator–Hygiene Theory** (see pp. 113–15)
- **Managerial grid** (see pp. 121–4)
- **Organic versus mechanistic management styles** (see pp. 169–72)
- **Related diversification grid** (see pp. 91–3)
- **The seven 'S's framework** (see pp. 181–5)

● **Situational leadership** (see pp. 131–4)

Main reference

G. Johnson and K. Scholes (1993), *Exploring Corporate Strategy*, London: Prentice Hall Int. (UK) Ltd.

31 Dynamics of paradigm change

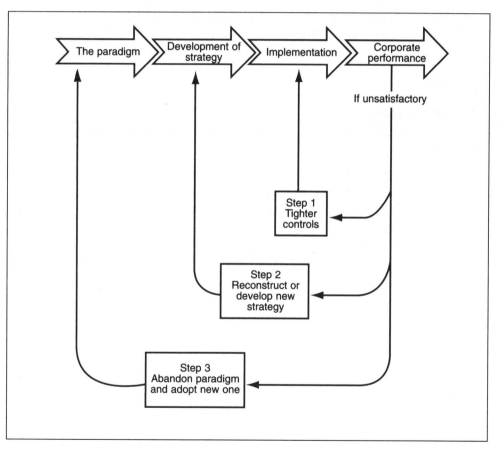

Source: *Turnabout: Managerial Recipes for Strategic Success*, P. Grinyer and J-C Spender, Associated Business Press.

Principle

The paradigm (recipe) may be changed by a set of dynamic processes.

Assumption

Managers resist strategic change that requires changing the paradigm itself. When faced with a need for strategic change – say, because of declining performance – they prefer incremental changes that do not involve changing the paradigm.

Elements

Paradigm/recipe
The paradigm comprises the key beliefs and assumptions forming part of an organization's culture.

- **Step 1**: Faced with declining performance or any stimulus for action for example, managers may first tighten controls.
- **Step 2**: If procedural controls are not effective, they may then reconstruct or develop a new strategy, but in line with the existing paradigm.
- **Step 3**: As a last resort they may seek to change the recipe or paradigm itself.

Issues

Resistance to change
Resisting change is often a way of attempting to avoid or reduce uncertainty or ambiguity.

Resistance to paradigm change
When imperative recipe change is resisted in favour of incremental change, environmental change outpaces strategic change which in

turn leads to strategic drift. For example, a change in the market brings a requirement for a new product range but the organization simply modifies existing products, failing to keep up with market demands.

The paradigm

Change at any level is most effective when consistent with the paradigm. The paradigm should be reappraised regularly to ensure that it reflects the organization's mission.

Cultural web

Items within the cultural web (see pp. 00–00) are normally changed before the paradigm is changed.

Application

Reinforcing the paradigm

The model encourages managers to continually reappraise the paradigm of the organization. It ensures that all changes are considered in the context of the recipe.

Prevention of drift

The model helps to prevent strategic drift caused through failure to keep pace with environmental change.

Level of change

The model ensures that required change is identified at the appropriate level – for example, a relocation rather than a refurbishment of existing accommodation.

Related models

- **Cultural web** (see pp. 141–4)
- **Five Ps for strategy** (see pp. 65–8)

- **Four organizational cultures** (see pp. 149–53)
- **M-O-S-T** (see pp. 161–3)
- **Organic versus mechanistic management styles** (see pp. 169–72)
- **The seven 'S's framework** (see pp. 181–5)

Main references

P. Grinyer and J-C. Spender (1979), *Turnabout: Managerial Recipes for Strategic Success*, London: Associated Business Press.

G. Johnson and K. Scholes (1993), *Exploring Corporate Strategy*, London: Prentice Hall Int. (UK) Ltd.

32 Four organizational cultures

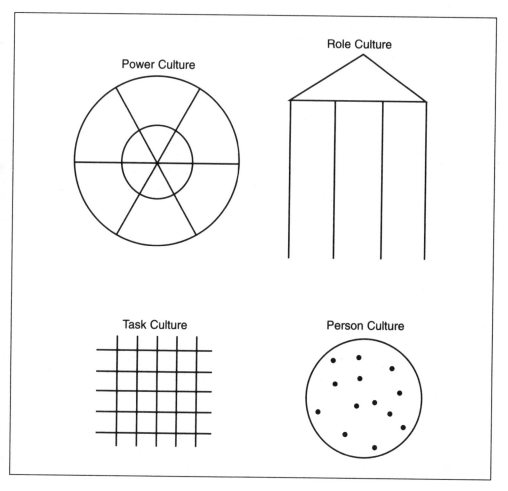

Source: *Understanding Organisations*, C. Handy, Penguin, Harmondsworth, 1976.
Copyright © Charles Handy, 1976, 1981, 1985, 1993.

Principle

There are four principal, identifiable types of culture in organizations.

Assumptions

It is possible to recognize those aspects of an organization which define its culture.

There are only four main types of culture.

Elements

Power culture
The power culture is a web with a central power source from which radiate circles of power and influence connected by specialist lines – for example, a small organization led by a strong entrepreneur.

Role culture
This is a culture characterized by a hierarchical, bureaucratic structure dependent upon functional or specialist departments (pillars) – for example, a government department.

Task culture
This is a job- or project-oriented culture where staff in different functions and on different levels freely interact. In this type of culture groups, project teams or task forces are formed for particular jobs – and is exemplified by the matrix organization.

Person culture
A person culture is typified by a group of individuals whose structure exists solely to service the individual members – for example, barristers' chambers or a kibbutz.

Issues

Power culture
The organization depends upon trust, empathy and personal conversation. Control is centralized. Since the web can break if it becomes too large, it is preferable to form other, linked organizations when building for growth.

Role culture
The work of the 'pillars', and their interaction, is controlled by procedures for roles, communications and settlement of disputes. Coordination is effected by a narrow band of senior management, the pediment. This culture is generally inflexible and slow to change.

Task culture
This culture is most effective where speed of reaction, integration, sensitivity and creativity are more important than depth of specialization. Its areas of difficulty lie in day-to-day control producing economies of scale and achieving great depth of expertise.

Person culture
Because this culture serves people's individual goals, control can only be achieved by mutual consent. These organizations are rare because conventional organizations have super-ordinate goals. Person cultures eventually develop their own identity and impose this on the individuals, thereby evolving into one of the other three cultural types.

Dominant power bases
There are different dominant power bases for each culture.

- **Power culture**: resource power
- **Role culture**: position power
- **Task culture**: expert power

- **Person culture**: expert or personal power

Applications

Assessment and appraisal
The model may be used to appraise the current culture with a view to developing a more appropriate one.

Interaction
The model may be used to consider the interaction of people, tasks and functions within an organization, and to understand the forces at work.

Joint ventures
The model may be used when assessing the cultural fit of one's own and other organizations – for example for a joint venture or merger.

Analysis tool
The model may be used as a descriptive tool for analysing typical organizational cultures in different industry sectors.

Related models

- **Belbin's team roles** (see pp. 105–8)
- **Cultural web** (see pp. 141–4)
- **Dynamics of paradigm change** (see pp. 145–8)
- **Group development** (see pp. 109–12)
- **Organic versus mechanistic management styles** (see pp. 169–72)
- **The seven 'S's framework** (see pp. 181–5)
- **Situational leadership** (see pp. 131–4)

Main reference

C.B. Handy (1985), *Understanding Organisations*, Harmondsworth: Penguin Books.

33 Integrated model of strategic management

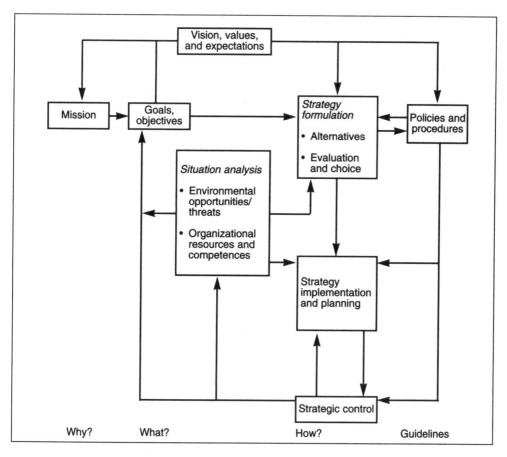

Source: *Strategic Management – Concepts, Decisions, Cases*, (2nd edn), Richard D. Irwin Inc.

Principle

There are different components to strategic planning and management which should be integrated.

Assumption

Strategic management is most effective when it is an integrated process.

Elements

This model integrates the process of effective strategic management through considering the following:

Why?
Why does the organization carry out certain activities (mission)?

What?
What should the organization do to achieve the mission (through its goals, objectives, vision, values, opportunities, threats, resources, competencies)?

How?
How may this be accomplished (alternatives, evaluation, strategy implementation and planning)?

Guidelines on implementation
These comprise the organization's policies and procedures.

Strategy
The strategy is the organization's preselected means of, or approach to, achieving its goals or objectives, while coping with current and future external conditions.

Mission
This is a broad statement providing a general direction for business activities and a basis for coherently selecting desired goals and objectives and the means to achieve them (strategies).

Goals
Goals are the broad objectives which the organization wishes to pursue or the results it wishes to accomplish within its mission.

Objectives
These are more specific ends to be met within the framework of the broader goals which involve specific time frames for accomplishment.

Issues

Centralization
If corporate development and coordination of individual businesses is the key objective, the company headquarters should formulate the strategy and accept that the motivation of unit managers and the performance of their units may suffer.

Delegation
Alternatively, if the financial performance of business units is critical, company headquarters should delegate strategy formulation to unit managers and accept less coordination between business units. Internal synergy may be increased through this integrated approach.

Difficulties in decision-making
Strategic decisions are rarely clear-cut or simple because:

- they rest upon intangibles and assumptions
- they involve value judgements, risks and uncertainties
- they usually involve high stakes
- long-term consequences are difficult to evaluate

- the organization may lack effective strategic decision-takers.

Applications

Strategy formulation
The model assists in the formulation of an integrated strategy for the organization and the evaluation of existing strategy against the integrated approach to identify weaknesses.

Delegation
The model helps to attribute decision-making roles to the most suitable managers.

Improving performance
By integrating strategic management, organizational performance can be improved through economies of scale, increased motivation of managers, enhanced working relationships, common usage of support functions and more effective communication processes and procedures.

Related models

- **Five forces** (see pp. 59–63)
- **Four routes to strategic advantage** (see pp. 69–72)
- **Geobusiness model** (see pp. 77–81)
- **M-O-S-T** (see pp. 161–3)
- **Nine specimen standardized strategies** (see pp. 201–5)
- **Patterns of strategic change** (see pp. 173–6)
- **PESTLIED** (see pp. 83–6)
- **The seven 'S's framework** (see pp. 181–5)
- **SWOT analysis** (see pp. 187–90)
- **Value chain** (see pp. 191–4)

Main reference

Lester A. Digman (1990), *Strategic Management – Concepts, Decisions, Cases*, (2nd edn), Richard D Irwin Inc.

34 M-O-S-T

Mission	WHAT	an organization is seeking to do
Objectives		
Strategy	HOW	an organization will achieve it
Tactics		

Principle

There are four stages in the effective development of an organization.

Assumption

A systematic approach to business development increases its long-term stability and effectiveness.

Elements

Mission
The mission is the organization's purpose and direction.

Objectives
Objectives are the organization's long-term goals.

Strategies
Strategies are the long-term plans designed to achieve the mission and objectives.

Tactics
Tactics are the short-term plans for implementing strategies.

Issues

Systematic development
An organization's development is most effective when carried out in a systematic and structured process.

Building strategy
An organization's development should start with a broad statement of purpose from which more detailed objectives and strategies are defined.

Purpose
All lower-level activities within an organization should further the higher-level purpose and direction.

Strategy setting
Many organizations successfully involve all levels of staff in the setting of the M-O-S-T elements.

Applications

Strategy
The model may be used to develop the organization's purpose and direction.

Focus
Organizations benefit from using the model to focus its resources.

Evaluation
The model provides a foundation for the evaluation of performance.

Motivation
Communication of M-O-S-T elements throughout the organization can help to integrate and motivate staff.

Goals
The model facilitates the prioritisation of goals.

Related models

- **Dynamics of paradigm change** (see pp. 145–8)
- **Integrated model of strategic management** (see pp. 155–9)
- **Nine specimen standardized strategies** (see pp. 201–5)
- **Organic versus mechanistic management styles** (see pp. 169–72)
- **Patterns of strategic change** (see pp. 173–6)
- **Porter's Diamond** (see pp. 87–90)
- **The seven 'S's framework** (see pp. 181–5)
- **Strategic triangle** (see pp. 95–8)
- **SWOT analysis** (see pp. 187–90)
- **Value chain** (see pp. 191–4)

Main reference

Not known.

35 Network analysis, PERT, CPA

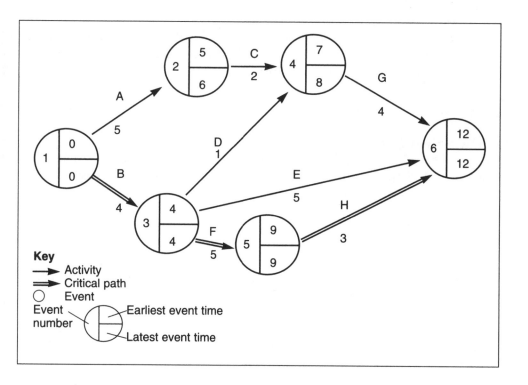

Principle

Network analysis is a technique used for planning large projects by rigorously programming and monitoring progress. It is the organized application of systematic reasoning for planning, scheduling, controlling and resourcing the many separate simultaneous or consecutive tasks making up a project.

There are two main types of network: precedence and activity-on-arrow networks. The latter is described below.

Assumptions

Network analysis accurately represents the real-life project to be controlled.

Programming and monitoring pinpoints the 'critical' parts of the project – that is, those parts that will have a significant impact on progress if not carried out as planned.

Elements

The network
The network is usually an activity-on-arrow diagram, representing each individual activity within a project with an arrowed line. Events are represented by circles or nodes.

The critical path
Each activity is allotted a certain amount of time. Project duration is the time taken to complete the longest path through the network. This is the 'critical path' and activities on it are 'critical activities'. The critical path is the 'bottleneck' route.

Float
Activities which do not lie on the critical path can, within limits, start late or take longer than specified. Slack time associated with a non-critical activity is its 'float'.

Issues

CPA and PERT
CPA (critical path analysis) and PERT (project evaluation and review technique) are forms of network analysis.

Critical path
Shortening the critical path may require consideration of both engineering problems and economic questions.

Crashing
It may be possible at extra expense to cut project time by assigning extra labour or equipment in order to shorten the time taken to complete certain jobs on the critical path. This is termed 'crashing'.

Resources
Resource allocation and Gantt charts permit estimating of the amount of resources required for a project. They can also be used for controlling, and showing the progress of, the project.

Uncertainty
In order to estimate activity times realistically, uncertainty should be analysed using a probability distribution for expected times.

Applications

Planning and control of projects
Network analysis may be used when planning and controlling large projects in fields such as construction, research and development and computerization.

Costs
The model may be used when comparing incremental costs and benefits.

Resource allocation
This refers to the allocation of resources, such as labour and equipment, in order to optimize costs over time and so minimize total project cost.

Project scheduling
This process includes, for example, budgeting and auditing procedures, product development and activity/event planning, such as military exercises.

Prioritization
CPA focuses attention on specific jobs that are critical to project time, helps determine the effects of shortening various jobs in the projects and enables the user to evaluate the costs of a 'crash' programme.

Related models

- **BCG matrix** (see pp. 51–4)
- **Net present value** (NPV) (see pp. 37–40)
- **Product life cycle** (see pp. 211–14)

Main reference

P.G. Moore and S.D. Hodges (1970), *Programming for Optimal Decisions, Part 2*, Harmondsworth: Penguin Books.
Readers who are interested in precedence networks should refer to:
J. Rodney Turner (1993), *The Handbook of Project-based Management* (part of Henley Management Series), London: McGraw-Hill.

36 Organic versus mechanistic management styles

Mechanistic	Organic
Specialized differentiation and definition of tasks in the organization	Contributive nature of special knowledge to the total concerns of the organization
Hierarchical supervision and reconciliation of problems	Redefinition of tasks and responsibilities through interaction with others
Precise definition of job responsibilities, methods, rights and obligations	Commitment to the organization beyond any technical/precise definition; such commitment more valued than loyalty
(Perceived) location of superior knowledge at the top of the hierarchy	Network structure of control, authority and communication
Vertical interaction of individuals between subordinate and superiors	Omniscience not imputed to senior executives; knowledge located anywhere in the organization and this location may become centre of authority for given issue
Insistence on loyalty to organization and obedience to superiors	
More prestige attached to job than to more general knowledge, experience and skills	Lateral, rather than vertical, direction of communication
	Communication consists of information and advice rather than instructions and decisions

Source: *The Management of Innovation*, T. Burns and G.M. Stalker, Tavistock Publications, 1961.

Principle

There are two principal contrasting management styles which are functions of the manager, the people they manage, the work activities, systems and the organizational culture.

Assumption

Managers and organizations can be classified into one of two broad categories. Organizations and their managements are mechanistic or organic, to varying degrees.

Elements

Mechanistic
The mechanistic management style is a bureaucratic approach to organization, based on clear structure, procedures, formal communications and controls.

Organic
With an organic management style the organization is based on fluid systems of management, flexible reporting lines, broad job descriptions, informal procedures and commitment of individuals to the organization's ethos.

Issues

Move to organic style
Currently organizations are generally moving from the mechanistic to organic management style as the increasing pace of change demands more flexibility and faster response.

Choice of style
There is no single best organizational style; particular circumstances

will dictate which is the most appropriate. For example, small, high technology organizations would normally benefit from an organic style whereas a large organization in a stable environment may benefit from some aspects of a mechanistic approach. The style of the organization may depend on its current state of health and prospects. In difficult circumstances, for instance, an organization may become more mechanistic.

Completely organic or mechanistic
No organization would be entirely organic or mechanistic.

Management style
To be most effective, the style of managers should match that of the unit or organization.

Applications

Assessment
The model provides a framework for assessing organizational and management styles.

Levels of use
The model may be applied at unit or function level. For example, a research and development unit would almost certainly benefit from an organic approach but with certain mechanistic features, such as rigorous cost control.

Audit checklist
The model provides a checklist of considerations for cultural audit and change.

Joint ventures
The model assists assessment of compatibility of organizations or units considering joint activities.

Matching styles

The model can help to identify a mismatch between the styles of a manager and the organization or business unit so that appropriate action such as redeployment or training, may be taken.

Related models

- **Cultural web** (see pp. 141–4)
- **Dynamics of paradigm change** (see pp. 145–8)
- **Financial ratios** (see pp. 29–32)
- **Five Ps for strategy** (see pp. 65–8)
- **Four organizational cultures** (see pp. 149–53)
- **Four routes to strategic advantage** (see pp. 69–72)
- **Job characteristics** (see pp. 117–20)
- **Maslow's hierarchy of needs** (see pp. 125–9)
- **M-O-S-T** (see pp. 161–3)
- **Patterns of strategic change** (see pp. 173–6)
- **Resource allocation at corporate level** (see pp. 177–80)
- **The seven 'S's framework** (see pp. 181–5)
- **Situational leadership** (see pp. 131–4)

Main references

G. Johnson and K. Scholes (1989), *Exploring Corporate Strategy*, London: Prentice Hall Int. (UK) Ltd.

T. Burns and G.M. Stalker (1961), *The Management of Innovation*, London: Tavistock.

37   Patterns of strategic change

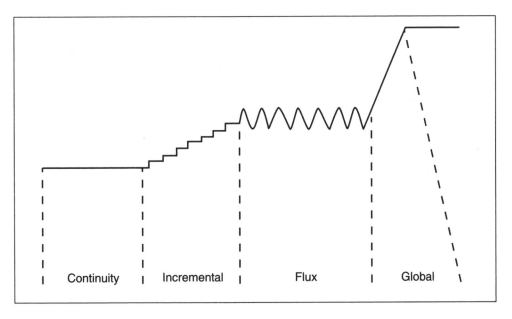

Continuity | Incremental | Flux | Global

Source: *Exploring Corporate Strategy* by G. Johnson and K. Scholes, Prentice Hall, London, 1989.

Principle

There are particular ways in which an organization's strategy tends to change.

Assumption

Once an organization has formulated a strategy it tends to develop from and within that strategy, rather than change its direction.

Elements

Continuity
This represents periods during which strategy remains unchanged.

Incremental
Strategies form gradually during this period.

Flux
Strategies change, but in no clear direction.

Global
This is a period of coordinated, strategic change throughout the organization, typically at times of crisis – for example, as a response to a decline in performance.

Issues

Continuity
Continuity is maintained where the defined strategy continues to be effective – for example in a relatively static environment.

Incremental change
Incremental change can be effective when in step with environmental change. When environmental change outpaces incremental change, global change may be necessary in order to 'catch up'.

Reactive change
Reactive changes in strategy can leave the organization literally in a

state of flux.

Anticipation of environmental change
Change strategies are normally more effective when made proactively in anticipation of environmental change.

Meaningless change
Change which has no clear justification (change for change's sake) is unlikely to contribute positively to the organization's development.

Applications

Systematic change
The model helps to ensure that strategic organizational change is a conscious and directed process.

Change facilitation
The model facilitates the selection of the pace and type of change of policy and procedures.

Evaluation
The model is an aid to the critical evaluation of particular change activities – for example, following a merger.

Selection of change
The model may be used to help define the type of change that may be most effective for a given organization. As certain types of organizations normally favour certain types of change, the nature of the organization (culture, paradigm) may be influenced by engineering the type and pace of change.

Related models

- **Five Ps for strategy** (see pp. 65–8)

- **Four routes to strategic advantage** (see pp. 69–72)
- **Integrated model of strategic management** (see pp. 55–9)
- **M-O-S-T** (see pp. 161–3)
- **Nine specimen standardized strategies** (see pp. 201–5)
- **Organic versus mechanistic management styles** (see pp. 169–72)
- **Product life cycle** (see pp. 211–14)
- **Resource allocation at corporate level** (see pp. 177–80)

Main references

G. Johnson and K. Scholes (1989), *Exploring Corporate Strategy*, London: Prentice Hall Int. (UK) Ltd.

H. Mintzberg (1978), 'Patterns of Strategy Formation', *Management Science*, May, pp. 934–48.

38 Resource allocation at corporate level

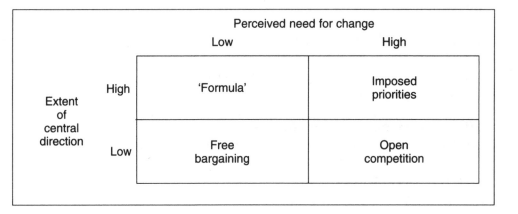

Source: *Exploring Corporate Strategy*, G. Johnson and K. Scholes, Prentice Hall, London, 1993.

Principle

Resources are allocated according to the degree of strategic change desired and corporate level intervention in the allocation process.

Assumption

The extent of corporate intervention in the allocation process is linked closely to the required degree of change in the resource base in order to effect desired strategic change.

Elements

Perceived need for change
This refers to change in the overall level of resources or in the deployment of those resources.

Extent of central direction
This refers to the degree of corporate level intervention in the allocation process.

Low perceived need for change
As corporate level intervention declines, resource allocation may move from a standard procedure ('formula') to a less structured allocation process.

High perceived need for change
As intervention declines, allocation will move from being highly directed ('imposed priorities') to becoming more competitive across different organizational units.

Issues

Formula allocation
If existing levels of resources and their deployment are unlikely to change, allocation is likely to proceed along historical lines ('formula').

Zero-based budgeting
Zero-based budgeting may mitigate the inflexibility of 'formula' allocations.

Growth
If new resources are allocated selectively, during growth, no business units need to be deprived.

Judging bids
The criteria for judging bids for resources must relate to the resources required to achieve organizational strategy.

Sharing resources
Sharing and duplication of resources by business units within the organization – for example, a shared personnel department – complicates the allocation process.

Political forces within the organization
Historically-based formula allocations may actually reflect the relative political strengths of different units rather than resource needs.

Understanding constraints
Unit managers must understand the constraints within which they are bargaining or bidding for resources.

Applications

Assessment
The model may be used to assess the allocation of resources depending on change characteristics.

Review
The model may be used to review the policy of central intervention.

Audit
Another use of the model is to audit the existing resource allocation process and recommend improvements – for example, to define and clarify resource allocation procedures.

Response to environmental change
The model can help in implementing the most effective resource allocation in response to environmental change.

Involvement of managers
The model can be used to implement and encourage unit manager involvement in the resource allocation process.

Related models

- **Organic versus mechanistic management styles** (see pp. 169–72)
- **Patterns of strategic change** (see pp. 173–6)
- **The seven 'S's framework** (see pp. 181–5)

Main reference

G. Johnson and K.Scholes (1993), *Exploring Corporate Strategy*, London: Prentice Hall Int. (UK) Ltd.

39 The seven 'S's framework

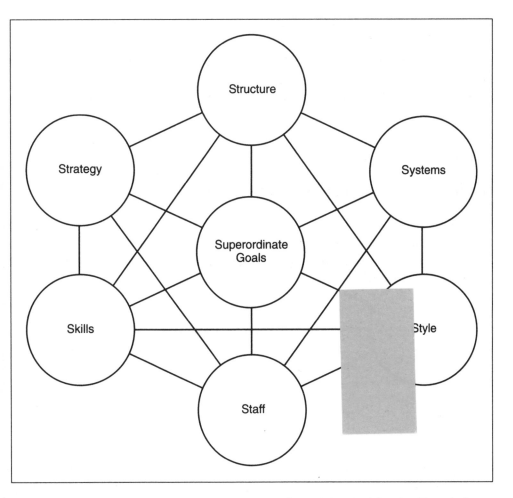

Reprinted from *Business Horizons*, June 1980. Copyright 1980 by the Foundation for the School of Business at Indiana University. Used with permission.

Principle

The model shows central, interconnected factors that influence the organization's effectiveness, especially its ability to change.

Assumptions

A change in one central factor can significantly affect another factor.

Effective change depends on the relationship between the elements of the model.

The pace of real change is geared to all seven elements, or factors, working together.

Elements

Seven factors interact to form the whole model.

Structure
This comprises the coordination of functions within the organization and emphasis on those parts which are most important to the organization's growth at any one time.

Strategy
This is an organization-planned response to, or anticipation of, changes in the external environment – for example, customers and competition.

Systems
Systems are the formal and informal procedures that enable the organization to operate.

Superordinate goals
These goals are the set of values or aspirations which act as guiding concepts, giving stability and meaning for staff.

Skills
Skills comprise the dominating attributes or capabilities of the organization.

Style
Style is the dominant patterns of action, including symbolic behaviour, by managers within the organization.

Staff
These are the human resources that can be developed and managed effectively.

Issues

Interdependence of factors
Most carefully planned strategies do not work because of inattention to the other factors. An organization is most effective when all the factors are coordinated.

Driving force for change
Any or all of the factors can be the driving force for change at any given time. The key is to focus on those factors that are currently most important to its evolution.

Systematic change
Systems is perhaps the most important factor within the model. Organizational change without disruption may be achieved most effectively by changing the systems. Even if structure and strategy are changed, the organization may remain ineffective until its supporting systems are aligned.

Importance of superordinate goals
Superordinate goals are absent in most organizations, but are evident in the superior performers.

Environmental change
An organization facing significant environmental change may need to dismantle an existing skills portfolio and add new skills.

Applications

Coordination
The model may be used to ensure that all the factors are coordinated to optimize conditions for growth or to consider the coordination of different organizational areas in times of change.

Prioritisation
The model can help to identify the factors which are most important at any one time.

Appraisal and audit
The model may be used when appraising or auditing organizations.

Related models

- **Belbin's team roles** (see pp. 105–8)
- **Contrasting characteristics of upstream and downstream companies** (see pp. 55–8)
- **Cultural web** (see pp. 141–4)
- **Dynamics of paradigm change** (see pp. 145–8)
- **Five Ps for strategy** (see pp. 65–8)
- **Four organizational cultures** (see pp. 149–53)
- **Integrated model of strategic management** (see pp. 155–9)
- **Maslow's hierarchy of needs** (see pp. 125–9)
- **M-O-S-T** (see pp. 161–3)
- **Organic versus mechanistic management styles** (see pp. 169–72)
- **Related diversification grid** (see pp. 91–3)
- **Situational leadership** (see pp. 131–4)

- **Strategic triangle** (see pp. 95–8)
- **SWOT analysis** (see pp. 189–90)

Main reference

H. Mintzberg and J.B. Quinn (1991), *The Strategy Process*, Englewood Cliffs, N.J.: Prentice Hall.

40 SWOT analysis

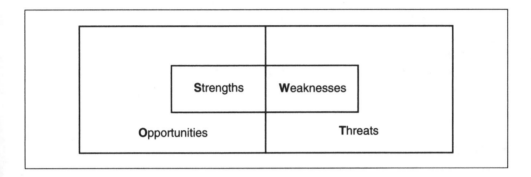

Principle

SWOT is a framework that can be used to evaluate a company or part of a company.

Assumption

The internal positive and negative attributes of an organization in relation to its external environment are central to its success.

Elements

Strengths
These comprise any positive internal attribute of the organization – for example, good cash flow, reputation or branding.

Weaknesses
These comprise any negative internal attribute of the organization – for example, obsolete technology or poor product/market mix.

Opportunities
Opportunities are the scope for taking advantage of external possibilities for growth – for example, a gap in the market or a new source of labour.

Threats
Threats are those external influences which can negatively impact on the organization's growth or health – for example, fiscal policy, new technology.

Issues

Context
SWOT analysis requires an understanding both of the organization's environment and of its resource capabilities.

Strengths
An organization can take advantage of strengths for future growth and can use them to better withstand adverse environmental forces – for example, competition.

Weaknesses
An organization may move away from activities that involve areas of weakness or may adopt a strategy to improve in weak areas.

Threats
What may be a threat for one organization would be seen as an opportunity for another – for example, the development of new production technology.

Analysis
The model tends to be used for qualitative analysis. Quantitative

evaluation enhances its value.

Other techniques
SWOT would normally be used as part of a process involving other analytical techniques.

Applications

Analysis

- of an existing organization or part of an organization
- of processes – for example, of the recruitment process
- of organizational problems as they arise.

Strategy formulation
SWOT analysis can be used in the development of organizational strategy.

Self-assessment
The model may also be used for individual's self-assessment.

Related models

- **Contrasting characteristics of upstream and downstream companies** (see pp. 55–8)
- **Demand and supply** (see pp. 17–20)
- **Financial ratios** (see pp. 29–32)
- **Four routes to strategic advantage** (see pp. 69–72)
- **Generic strategies** (see pp. 73–6)
- **Geobusiness model** (see pp. 77–81)
- **Integrated model of strategic management** (see pp. 155–9)
- **M-O-S-T** (see pp. 161–3)
- **Nine specimen standardized strategies** (see pp. 201–5)
- **The seven 'S's framework** (see pp. 181–5)
- **Strategic triangle** (see pp. 95–8)

Main reference

G. Johnson and K. Scholes (1989), *Exploring Corporate Strategy*, London: Prentice Hall Int. (UK) Ltd.

41 Value chain

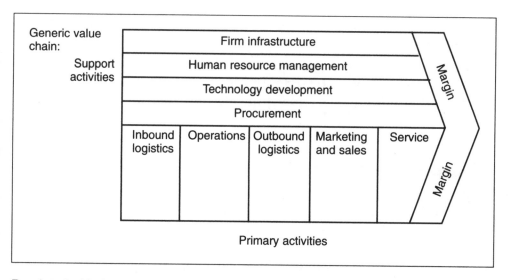

Generic value chain:

Support activities

Firm infrastructure
Human resource management
Technology development
Procurement

Margin

Inbound logistics | Operations | Outbound logistics | Marketing and sales | Service

Margin

Primary activities

Principle

The model shows how the activities of an organization can help to contribute to the value offered to customers through products and services.

Assumption

Every function and activity, and how they interrelate, can improve an organization's competitive position.

Elements

Primary activities

- inbound logistics (storage, reception, internal storage)
- operations (transforming inputs into products)
- outbound logistics (collection, storage, distribution)
- marketing and sales
- service

Support activities

- procurement
- technology, plant and equipment
- human resource management (recruitment, development, reward)
- infrastructure (planning, finance, legal, management)

Value

The value chain displays total potential value which equals value activities plus profit margin.

Issues

Customers' perception of value

Value should be defined from the customer's viewpoint.

Adding value

The interface and synergy between different activities is often a crucial determinant of the potential for adding value.

Analysis
An organization's value chain may be analysed in relation to value activities outside the organization, such as suppliers and product distribution.

Specificity
The model will have to be adapted to take account of the specific functions and activities of a particular organization.

Applications

Exploiting competitive advantage
Value chain analysis can help to determine areas of competitive advantage. For example, managers may assess links between activities or functions and identify potential synergies in order to optimise performance.

Identifying opportunities for integration
Activities may be assessed to identify opportunities for forward integration into client value chains – for example, joint training or environmental audit activities, product development and research.

Better understanding customer needs
Customer value chain activities may be analysed to better understand customer requirements.

Analysing competitors' strengths and weaknesses
Competitors' value chains may be analysed to determine their strengths and weaknesses, which may then be exploited.

Identifying potential partners
Examining value chains can help to identify potential partners for joint ventures.

Related models

- **BCG matrix** (see pp. 51–4)
- **Company position/industry attractiveness screen** (see pp. 137–40)
- **Contrasting characteristics of upstream and downstream companies** (see pp. 55–8)
- **Financial ratios** (see pp. 29–32)
- **Integrated model of strategic management** (see pp. 155–9)
- **M-O-S-T** (see pp. 161–3)
- **Resource allocation at corporate level** (see pp. 177–80)

Main references

M.E. Porter (1985), *Competitive Advantage: Creating and Sustaining Superior Performance*, New York: The Free Press.

M.E. Porter (1980), *Competitive Strategy: Techniques for Analyzing Industries and Competitors*, New York: The Free Press.

Strategic marketing

42   Ansoff's Box

	Current products	New products
Current markets	Market penetration	Product development
New markets	Market development	Diversification

Source: *Corporate strategy*, rev. edn, I. Ansoff, McGraw-Hill, New York, 1987.

Principle

Particular general growth strategies can be recommended, given particular prevailing product and market states.

Assumption

New products and new markets require different growth strategies from current (established) products and markets.

Elements

Market penetration
Efforts are directed towards increasing market share.

Market development strategy
New markets are developed for current products.

Product development
Existing products are developed in some way for current markets.

Diversification
Completely new products are developed or acquired.

Issues

Dynamics
In using this model it is important to consider the dynamics in the relationship between product development and the potential size and nature of the markets.

Competition
The competitive advantage of the firm and the product must be considered in relation to their market positioning.

Synergy
Synergy should be explored to identify opportunities for the development of complementary, new or existing product–market activities.

Applications

Strategy development
This model may be used to analyse the product portfolio to help

develop an appropriate marketing strategy. For example, a company may decide to penetrate a market by encouraging competitors' customers to switch brands.

Encouraging growth
An organization could apply this model to its product portfolio to determine how the combination of product and market developments might contribute to business growth.

Other uses
The model shown pictorially may be used with different axes such as current and new strategies versus current and new markets, or current and new strategies versus current and new products.

Related models

- **BCG matrix** (see pp. 51–4)
- **Company position/industry attractiveness screen** (see pp. 137–40)
- **Five forces** (see pp. 59–63)
- **Product life cycle** (see pp. 211–14)

Main references

H.I. Ansoff (1965), *Corporate Strategy*, (rev. edn 1987), New York: McGraw-Hill Inc.

H.I. Ansoff, R.P. Declerck and R.L. Hayes (1976), *From Strategic Planning to Strategic Management*, New York: John Wiley.

H.I. Ansoff (1984), *Implementing Strategic Management*, Englewood Cliffs, N.J.: Prentice-Hall International.

43 Nine specimen standardized strategies

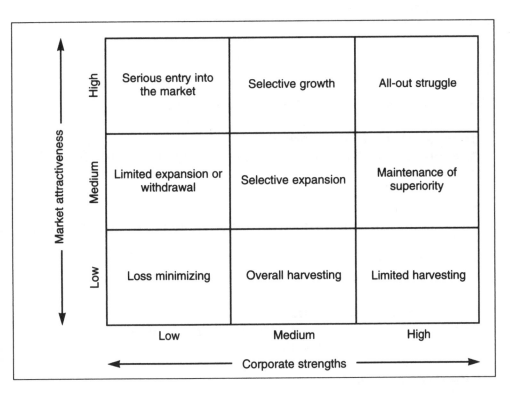

Source: *The Mind of the Strategist (The Art of Japanese Business)*, K. Ohmae, McGraw-Hill, Maidenhead, 1982. Reproduced with the permission of the McGraw-Hill Companies.

Principle

It is possible to define Standardized strategies based on market characteristics and organizational strengths.

Assumption

Market attractiveness and organizational strength are critical variables on which strategy depends.

Elements

The model suggests nine standardized marketing strategies.

Serious entry into the market
A favourable market is entered, and quickly withdrawn from if not viable.

Selective growth
Investments are concentrated where advantage can be maintained.

All-out struggle
Effort is concentrated on maintaining strength and profit structure.

Limited expansion or withdrawal
Attractive, low-risk, expansion opportunities are sought, withdrawing if unsuccessful.

Selective expansion
The organization expands in profitable, low-risk segments.

Maintenance of superiority
Productivity is improved whilst avoiding large-scale investment.

Loss minimizing
Fixed costs are minimized and investment avoided, rapidly withdrawing when loss is unavoidable.

Overall harvesting
Profitability is emphasized by switching from fixed to variable costs.

Limited harvesting
Profitability is protected even if loss of market position is involved.

Issues

Business units
The model has been developed to focus on different business units within an organisation, recognizing that different strategies may be appropriate in the various units.

Unit attributes
The informal attributes of a unit should be considered, including creativity, persistence and imagination, in addition to the formal attributes such as finance and product portfolio.

Interaction of units
The interaction of units, given their possible diverse strategies, should be carefully considered.

Applications

Strategy formulation
The model may be used to formulate strategy of different business units within an organization, or companies within a group, given their particular strengths and market position.

Strategy review
Strategy can be reviewed as a company's or unit's strengths or market attractiveness changes.

Portfolio analysis
The portfolio of different companies or units can be analysed with a view to adopting a more attractive balance through appropriate acquisitions or other growth initiatives.

Repositioning
A company's or unit's position on the matrix may be assessed with a view to repositioning through influencing market attractiveness or corporate strengths.

Related models

- **Barriers and profitability** (see pp. 47–50)
- **Company position/industry attractiveness screen** (see pp. 137–40)
- **Contrasting characteristics of upstream and downstream companies** (see pp. 55–8)
- **Economies of scale** (see pp. 21–4)
- **Five forces** (see pp. 59–63)
- **Four routes to strategic advantage** (see pp. 69–72)
- **Generic strategies** (see pp. 73–6)
- **Geobusiness model** (see pp. 77–81)
- **Integrated model of strategic management** (see pp. 155–9)
- **M-O-S-T** (see pp. 161–3)
- **Patterns of strategic change** (see pp. 173–6)
- **PESTLIED** (see pp. 83–6)
- **Porter's Diamond** (see pp. 87–90)
- **Product life cycle** (see pp. 211–14)
- **Strategic triangle** (see pp. 95–8)
- **SWOT analysis** (see pp. 187–90)

Main reference

K. Ohmae (1982), *The Mind of the Strategist (The Art of Japanese Business)*, New York: McGraw-Hill.

44 PIMS competitive strategy paradigm

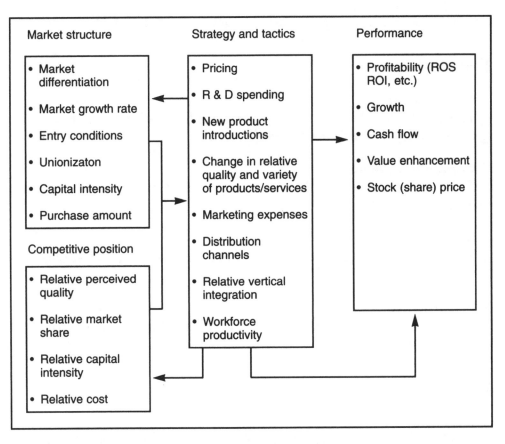

Market structure

- Market differentiation
- Market growth rate
- Entry conditions
- Unionizaton
- Capital intensity
- Purchase amount

Competitive position

- Relative perceived quality
- Relative market share
- Relative capital intensity
- Relative cost

Strategy and tactics

- Pricing
- R & D spending
- New product introductions
- Change in relative quality and variety of products/services
- Marketing expenses
- Distribution channels
- Relative vertical integration
- Workforce productivity

Performance

- Profitability (ROS ROI, etc.)
- Growth
- Cash flow
- Value enhancement
- Stock (share) price

Adapted with the permission of The Free Press, a division of Simon & Schuster from *THE PIMS PRINCIPLE: Linking Strategy to Performance* by Robert D. Buzzell and Bradley T. Gale. Copyright © 1987 by The Free Press.

Principle

PIMS is the Profit Impact of Market Strategy, a research study which assessed the key variables affecting profit.

Assumption

Three principal factors define an organization's performance: strategy, competitive position and market/industry characteristics.

Elements

Market structure
These are the factors in the marketplace which influence the organization's ability to succeed.

Competitive position
This refers to the strength of the organization in the market, relative to its competitors.

Strategy and tactics
These are the broad range of factors defining the organization's direction.

Performance
Performance is represented by quantifiable indicators of achievement.

Issues

Linkages
Market structure, competitive position and strategy and tactics are interdependent and affect performance. Market share and profitability are strongly related. Most strategic factors that boost

return on investment also contribute to long-term shareholder value.

Performance
In the long term the single most important factor affecting performance is product/service quality relative to competitors' quality. Market leaders command higher prices and maintain their leadership position by offering products and services that are superior relative to those offered by their competitors.

Cash generation
In practice, many 'dog' and 'question mark' businesses generate cash; many 'cash cows' do not.

Other issues
Selling price inflation, degree of product/service standardization and the extent of industry exports and imports are also important issues.

Applications

Strategy
The model may be applied in the assessment and formulation of strategy.

Manipulation of variables
The model can help to identify the most important variables affecting performance and assess their interdependence. Performance may then be improved through influencing variables – for example, by increasing effective marketing spend.

Product portfolio
The model may assist in the evaluation and development of an improved product portfolio.

Related models

- **Company position/industry attractiveness screen** (see pp. 137–40)
- **Elasticity** (see pp. 25–8)
- **Four routes to strategic advantage** (see pp. 69–72)
- **PESTLIED** (see pp. 83–6)
- **Porter's Diamond** (see pp. 87–90)
- **Related diversification grid** (see pp. 91–3)
- **Strategic triangle** (see pp. 95–8)

Main reference

R.D. Buzzell and B.T. Gale (1987), *The PIMS Principle – Linking Strategy to Performance*, New York: The Free Press.

45 Product life cycle

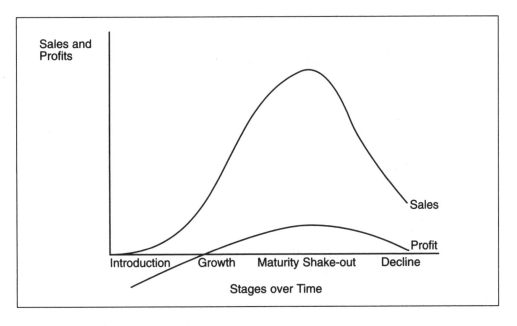

Source: Marketing Management, 8/e by Kotler, Philip. Reprinted by permission of Prentice-Hall Inc., Upper Saddle River, NJ.

Principle

This model illustrates how sales and profit vary during the life of a product.

Assumption

Products have a typical pattern of identifiable stages, forming the life cycle.

Elements

Product development stage
Heavy investment, market research and idea generation take place at this stage.

Introduction stage
Product launch with slow sales growth is accompanied by losses.

Growth stage
There is significantly increased market demand and a move into profit.

Maturity stage
There is a slow down, possibly leading to a decline in sales. Stable or reducing profits are expected.

Shake-out stage
There may be a shake-out amongst competitors, during which some may withdraw and others may become stronger.

Decline stage
This is typified by a significant reduction in sales and profits.

Issues

Product life
The longevity of different products varies greatly from fad products, such as skateboards possibly lasting just a season, to established products, such as televisions, with a life of many years.

Pattern of life cycle

The pattern of the life cycle varies between products and may contain more complex characteristics than the typical form. For example, several peaks and troughs could indicate varying demand over time, or the entry of the product into new market segments.

Product shake-out

Between the growth and maturity stages the market is saturating and the relative strengths of competitors becomes important, often leading to a shake-out in the number of products.

Product strategy

The approach taken during each stage of the life cycle depends on the nature of the organization's product strategy – for example, rapid versus slow market penetration – or the need for market testing before further development.

Applications

Analysis of individual products

The model can be applied to individual products such as a particular car model, brands (for example, a type of car), classes of products (cars) and technologies (petrol-fuelled engines).

Analysis of assets and processes

The model may be used to describe not just the life of individual products but, for example, the fate of a significant item of plant, a process or a strategy, such as a particular marketing strategy, thus predicting its likely progress.

Linking marketing to other functions

Each stage of the life cycle requires a different approach to marketing and other organizational functions. For example, during the introduction life cycle stage, promotion might be high; during growth new distribution channels may be introduced; during maturity a decision should be made about the future of the product (for example, product modification); and, during decline, product relaunch or phase-out may be considered.

Related models

- **Ansoff's Box** (see pp. 197–9)
- **BCG matrix** (see pp. 51–4)
- **Economies of scale** (see pp. 21–4)
- **Five forces** (see pp. 59–63)
- **Network analysis, PERT, CPA** (see pp. 165–8)
- **Nine specimen standardized strategies** (see pp. 201–5)
- **Patterns of strategic change** (see pp. 173–6)
- **PESTLIED** (see pp. 83–6)

Main references

P. Kotler (1988), *Marketing Management* (6th edn), Englewood Cliffs, N.J.: Prentice Hall.
A.D. Little (1974) *A System of Managing Diversity.*

Appendix

Appendix: Effective thinking processes and the use of management models

Management models can appear to be very simple, so that we select and use them without sufficient consideration. However, this can be deceptive, leading to their inappropriate application, which in turn can restrict rather than develop our thinking and analysis. When developing our understanding of organizational activities, and their environment, we need to be rigorous in our selection and application of models. Understanding organizations themselves is, of course, critical here, although we will be much more effective in this process if we have some appreciation of the psychology of thinking, learning and developing understanding.

Models can help us to clarify, broaden and deepen our analysis and thinking and to organize, manage and manipulate reality in our minds. An awareness of thinking processes is crucial if we are to do this effectively.

Theory of thinking and learning

As, from birth, we develop our ability to think, we move from concrete thinking, based on sensory information from the environment, to more abstract thinking, based on concepts, associations and inferences. In this section we shall summarize some theory first, and then relate this to management, organizations and the application of models.

When we see or hear, or in some other way sense, what is going on around us, the information is filtered through a process of perception.

Our thinking is, then, influenced not by actual reality but by perceived reality. As different people will, to some degree, perceive the same object or situation differently, their response to it will be different. Experiences of long meetings in organizations clearly supports this. Perception is therefore a process of interpretation, and is influenced by our knowledge, experience, motives, values and other individual attributes. Management models help to reduce the variations caused by perception. However, there will inevitably be differences in the interpretation of analyses by different people. Understanding this, we should seek to be as objective as possible in the use of models, whilst recognizing the complex breadth of issues that can affect our interpretation of analyses.

As we think, we represent reality in our minds using different, interrelated forms of images. For example, when considering an organization we may picture the physical organization, people and, possibly, activities. This may be accompanied by feelings and emotional responses.

Young children's, or immature, thinking is restricted to the immediate and to real, 'concrete' objects. Advanced thinking is able to manipulate ideas about objects. Thinking on the basis of abstractions of objects – dealing with symbols and ideas about the world, not just about the world itself – therefore develops. At this level of thinking, people can implicitly organize and manipulate reality in their minds, dealing with theoretical issues, the future, imagined and new, or creative, events. The ability to infer develops with this level of complex thinking. Inference is the ability to consider causal relationships and alternative explanations for a given set of circumstances or events. Problem solving can be carried out mentally by tracing linkages between different related ideas or issues.

The use of management models to analyse organizational and business events, processes and systems develops from this advanced level of thinking. Models help us to abstract from reality the fundamental issues which we can then mentally organize and manipulate to help in developing depth of understanding and inferring what will happen in the future, for effective problem solving and in creative thinking.

Concepts

We think in concepts. A concept is an abstraction of more than one event or objects which are perceived to have something in common. It is therefore a generalization about an object or event. For example, at a simple level of abstraction, we soon learn the general, common characteristics of a pen so that we can then recognize an object as a pen even though we have never seen that particular pen before. At a complex level, an adult can recognize forces affecting an organization from the environment and classify them, by abstraction, as being, for example, political, social or economic.

Although this level of thinking is complex, abstraction and conceptual thinking, and classifying objects and processes, help us to make sense of the complexity in an organization or its environment, through simplifying complexity and organizing the issues or elements. By their nature, management models are generalized abstractions of reality, based on concepts developed from common characteristics. Simplifying and generalizing activities and processes into management models allows us to develop common approaches to analyses and a common understanding and language with which to describe organizations.

However, abstraction and generalization into concepts does have disadvantages. It can cause us to develop biased thinking, by always attributing the same and full set of characteristics to all objects of the same, defined type, without taking account of individual differences. Further, if we assume that our conceptual model, or management model, is complete in itself, we can actually restrict our thinking rather than make it more effective. For example, an organization defined as a bureaucracy may be immediately perceived as slow, impersonal, hierarchical and procedural without taking account of that organization's particular characteristics. We must therefore guard against allowing our conceptualizations to form judgements on the basis of limited evidence. We should critically assess the generalizations and development of conceptual elements in management models so that we become aware of the degree to which they simplify reality and to ensure they do not overgeneralize or develop bias in our analysis.

Application of theory in the use of management models

From this discussion, some principles and cautions can be derived for the application of models in the analysis of organizational and management issues.

The development of management models is a direct response to our natural process of abstraction, generalization and conceptualization as we try to simplify complexity in organizations and in the environment.

Organizations and management processes are very complex, containing many interacting concrete and abstract objects and processes. We should take an integrated approach when we analyse organizations and not allow models to create too narrow a focus.

By simplifying organizational objects and processes into concepts, and in the development of management models, we must take care not to oversimplify or overgeneralize, thereby missing both deeper complex issues and issues which are specific to an organization. A model must always, therefore, be treated as an incomplete and imperfect representation of reality.

Many activities or processes in organizations cannot be objectively measured. We can assess them using rigorous research techniques but we normally rely heavily on subjective judgement. Perceptual processes cause us, therefore, to strongly interpret reality. Because of this, we must recognize that, even though we may use what seem to be well formed, scientific models to analyse an organization, different people may interpret the same situation differently and may therefore arrive at different conclusions and recommendations after using the same models.

Our wider experience, our perceptual filters and the use of management models could develop bias and inappropriate focus in our analysis of a particular organization. We should continuously step back and consider broader issues and other possible interpretations.

Mental processing

The design of many of the models reproduced in this book conforms to the way in which we store and manipulate information in our brains. By understanding mental processes, and how management models are consistent with these, we can become more effective and efficient in our thinking and in using management models to enhance creativity in organizational and business analysis. Again, we will explore some theory first.

Our brains are made up of thousands of millions of interconnected neurones. The number of possible paths of connections is so great that we can consider the capacity of our brains to be virtually limitless. Information in our brains links to form breadth and depth of related knowledge. A network of related information forms what can be termed a 'mental model'. The process of understanding is essentially the process of linking different 'bits' of information. When we do not understand some new information, it is because we do not have an existing mental model with which to link this information.

Creative thinking and problem solving involves linking existing information in new ways and therefore developing new ideas. As representations of mental models, management models can be used to enhance mental analysis, creative thinking and problem solving.

The brain is divided into two halves – right and left. Research has shown that, in general, the left side of the brain carries out those mental activities including logic, sequence, analysis, words and numbers ('scientific' thinking) and the right side of the brain generally carries out activities relating to rhythm, colour, dimension and images ('artistic' thinking). The Western education system has evolved to place greater value on left-brain thinking. However, the most effective and creative thinking develops when we use both sides of our brain. The use of management models, as visual representations, generally increases the use of the right side of the brain.

Research has also shown that certain conditions improve thinking and understanding. Information that is linked to form a bigger picture will be recalled better than discrete pieces of information. Unusual or novel events, or information associated in some way with these, will be recalled better than expected or 'normal' events. Learning is improved when information is received through more than one sense. Also, when we take breaks and information is reviewed, we give time for the brain to reorganize the information and integrate it in new ways, finding more linkages, developing mental models and deepening understanding.

Application to management models

From our understanding of the way we process and organize information we can consider how best to use management models to analyse an organization or management situation, and how to study and write assignments if we are students.

With our knowledge of mental processing, it is clear, in our use of management models, that the more we are able to manipulate information, critically assess its relevance, consider links with other concepts and models and use different ways to represent reality and present the information, the more effective will be our understanding about organizational and management processes.

Models should be used as tools in analyses and never as ends in themselves. We should start with the organizational problem, not with the model that we think we should apply. We should use models to break down a problem domain or analysis into manageable chunks that we can then manipulate and develop in our thinking into meaningful internal conceptual associations, or mental models.

To this end, management models should be internalized mentally before we use them. Our thinking will always be more effective if we can manipulate elements of a model in our minds before we seek to use them on paper.

We will also be more effective in the use of models if we read around their original development. This will provide the contextual information we need to internalize, understand and develop mental models, and on which to build a clear and effective analytical approach.

We should use management models to help us order and link information and elements of organization-related activities and processes. We need to think clearly about the way the different model elements relate and the factors which influence these relationships.

We can improve strategic analysis by trying to develop new linkages between elements in a model, or between models, without losing their integrity. By finding new links which are not explicit in models we can increase understanding and produce creative ways of carrying out organizational and management analysis and development.

We can improve our thinking and understanding by employing approaches to problem solving which use both sides of our brains. The visual representation often used for models will enhance the processing carried out in the right side. During analysis, the use of both sides of the brain will also be enhanced by using, for example, colour, pictures and shapes as well as lists and flowcharts.

We will improve our concentration and understanding if we adopt certain approaches to analysis and study. We should take regular five-minute breaks – say, every 30 minutes – from concentrated analysis. We should spend time reviewing important issues, reinforcing them and finding links with other concepts and ideas. We should try to build new information on to existing concepts or mental models, developing an integrated picture of the whole area of analysis. This is especially important for strategic analysis. When we find an issue which is of particular importance, this should be marked and emphasized in some way. In the mind this may be by association with a particular image or on paper, using colour or difference in size. Finally, we should develop different ways of making notes. Mind-mapping is particularly effective for organizing information, analysis and defining links between different elements on paper or computer, and is consistent with the way in which many management models are presented.

Subject index

A Systematic Approach to
Getting Results

Surya Lovejoy

Every manager has to produce results. But almost nobody is trained in the business of doing so. This book is a practical handbook for making things happen. And whether the thing in question is a conference, an office relocation or a sales target, the principles are the same: you need a systematic approach for working out:

- exactly what has to happen
- when everything has to happen
- how you will ensure that it happens
- what could go wrong
- what will happen when something does go wrong
- how you will remain sane during the process.

This book won't turn you into an expert on critical path analysis or prepare you for the job of running the World Bank. What it will do is to give you the tools you need to produce results smoothly, effectively, reliably and without losing your mind on the way.

Gower

Gower Handbook of Management Skills

Third Edition

Edited by Dorothy M Stewart

'This is the book I wish I'd had in my desk drawer when I was first a manager. When you need the information, you'll find a chapter to help; no fancy models or useless theories. This is a practical book for real managers, aimed at helping you manage more effectively in the real world of business today. You'll find enough background information, but no overwhelming detail. This is material you can trust. It is tried and tested.'

So writes Dorothy Stewart, describing in the preface the unifying theme behind the new edition of this bestselling *Handbook*. This puts at your disposal the expertise of 25 specialists, each a recognized authority in their particular field. Together, this adds up to an impressive 'one stop library' for the manager determined to make a mark.

Chapters are organised within three parts: Managing Yourself, Managing Other People, and Managing Business. Part I deals with personal skills and includes chapters on self-development and information technology. Part II covers people skills such as listening, influencing and communication. Part III looks at finance, project management, decision-making, negotiating and creativity. A total of 12 chapters are completely new, and the rest have been rigorously updated to fully reflect the rapidly changing world in which we work.

Each chapter focuses on detailed practical guidance, and ends with a checklist of key points and suggestions for further reading.

Gower

The Management Skills Book

Conor Hannaway and Gabriel Hunt

From managing employee performance to chairing meetings, and from interviewing staff to making retirement presentations, the list of skills demanded of today's manager seems endless. How can you be effective in all these areas?

If you are a practising manager, this book is for you. It is designed to answer your need for support in your day-to-day work.

Over 100 brief guides cover essential management skills. Each guide gives you all you need to know without cumbersome technical details. Look up the subject you need, and apply the ideas immediately.

The Management Skills Book was written with today's busy managers in mind. It is an ideal introduction for new managers, and a great reminder of the essentials for the more experienced.

Gower

Superboss 2

The New A-Z of Managing People Successfully

David Freemantle

You too can be a SUPERBOSS!

David Freemantle will persuade you that every manager can take action today to become a SUPERBOSS. In this entertaining book, a revised and updated version of a worldwide bestseller, he describes more than 130 effective ways of managing people.

Amusing, stimulating and often provocative, *Superboss 2* is a treasure trove of practical advice for anyone aspiring to managerial excellence.

Gower